6502 Machine Code for Humans

6502 Machine Code for Humans

Alan Tootill and David Barrow

GRANADA
London Toronto Sydney New York

Granada Technical Books
Granada Publishing Ltd
8 Grafton Street, London W1X 3LA

First published in Great Britain by
Granada Publishing 1984

British Library Cataloguing in Publication Data
Tootill, Alan
6502 machine code for humans.
1. 6502 (Microprocessor)—Programming
2. Machine codes (Electronic computers)
I. Title   II. Barrow, David
001.64′25   QA76.8.S63

ISBN 0-246-12076-2

Typeset by V & M Graphics Ltd, Aylesbury, Bucks
Printed and bound in Great Britain by
Mackays of Chatham, Kent

Contents

Preface

Machine code is the language of the processor at the heart of your computer system. As its name suggests, it is a language designed for a machine to use. But the language and the machine are both products of human minds and machine code is just as much a language for humans.

Unlike many other books on machine code, this book does not systematically explain the operation of each instruction in excessive detail. Instead, it presents you with simple, understandable tasks in computing that are carried out by groups of instructions (routines). Each task is described, the method explained and sufficient documentation given for you to work through the routines and see the part played by each instruction. Just as the words of a natural language come alive only in phrases and sentences, the instructions in a machine language have meaning only in how they relate to a complete process.

We do not expect you to find this an easy or superficial book. Learning any language is hard work and, perhaps, machine code is more so than others since it demands attention to absolutely precise detail. But the effort has its rewards. On the practical side, a knowledge of machine code will enable you to understand more about the way your computer works and so put it to more effective use. On the recreational side – and we are dealing with *personal* computers, not the company mainframe – writing machine code that will directly control every action your computer makes can be as satisfying and pleasurable as playing chess or solving crossword puzzles. Writing better, more efficient code is a challenge to the intellect; machine code is habit-forming.

We would like to thank Richard Miles and the staff of Granada Publishing for their patience and fine efforts with the manuscript, also our families who accepted our preoccupation with fortitude. Not least, we wish to thank the contributors to our machine code series *PCW SUB SET* in the British magazine, *Personal Computer World*, whose enthusiasm for machine code programming encouraged us to write this book.

Alan Tootill
David Barrow

Chapter One
Getting Started

When a personal computer is switched on, the processor automatically carries out a cycle of fetching and executing instructions that are stored in the computer's memory. Only instructions of a limited form known as *machine code* are recognised by the processor. Any other form of instruction, such as that encountered in a BASIC program, has to be converted into equivalent machine code for execution, either in advance by a program called a *compiler*, or whilst running by a program called an *interpreter*.

Computer codes, representing instructions and data, are *binary* numbers, usually expressed in the more convenient *hexadecimal* notation. Appendix B gives a brief explanation of these number systems as well as 2's complement and binary coded decimal (BCD).

Since even hexadecimal codes are difficult to use, machine code programming is usually done with the aid of a program called an *assembler* which converts easily remembered instruction *mnemonics* into actual machine code. Assemblers allow you to enter and edit instructions in mnemonic form and to use labels for branch and subroutine call destinations, calculating the addresses for you. If you insert or delete instructions, the source code (mnemonics) can be reassembled into machine code, the assembler taking care of all address changes. *Hand-assembly* is the process of carrying out the functions of an assembler by hand – tedious but necessary if you do not have an assembler. In Appendix A, and throughout the book, we give assembler mnemonics alongside the machine code.

The 6502 processor

As far as the software writer is concerned, the 6502 processor consists of one 16-bit register, five 8-bit registers and internal logic which deals with arithmetic and data movement.

The 16-bit register is used by the processor as a pointer to the memory location where the next instruction will be found. Three of the 8-bit registers are accessible to the programmer for storing values (0 to 255), carrying out arithmetic, acting as loop counters, and so on. The fourth is really a collection of 8 single bits (flags) giving certain information about processes carried out. The fifth 8-bit register is the stack pointer which indexes a reserved area of RAM called the *stack*. Use of the stack is explained below.

The internal logic which decodes instructions need not concern us. Provided the processor is fed with the correct data and the right instructions in the right order, it will do the job we want. We do have to know how to make the processor act on data in specified memory locations using the correct addressing mode.

Fuller information about the 6502 registers, flags and addressing modes is given in Appendix A where it is handy for quick reference.

The 6502 stack

The 6502 stack occupies page 1 of memory (addresses $0100 to $01FF) and is used primarily for storage of the current program address when a subroutine is called. It is also used for temporary storage of register contents while the registers are used for other purposes.

The stack is indexed by the 8-bit stack pointer. When the computer is switched on this takes a random value and has to be initialised via the X register using the TXS instruction. The usual initialisation value is $FF – the highest stack address. Thereafter the stack pointer will keep track of the next stack location available for storage of an 8-bit value.

JSR (jump to subroutine) causes a sequence of four actions affecting the stack and stack pointer (S).

(1) The high order byte of the Program Counter (PC) is copied to stack at $0100+S.
(2) S is decreased by 1 to point to the next free stack location.
(3) The low order byte of the PC is copied to $0100+S.
(4) S is again decreased by 1.

The PC is then loaded with the subroutine address from the JSR instruction and execution continues at the subroutine. At the end of the subroutine, the instruction RTS (return from subroutine) causes the reverse sequence:

(1) S is increased by 1.
(2) Lo-byte PC is loaded from $0100+S.
(3) S is increased by 1.
(4) Hi-byte PC is loaded from $0100+S.

PC is increased by 1 and program execution then continues from the instruction following the JSR.

Register values can also be saved (pushed) to and restored (pulled) from stack using the PHA, PHP, PLA and PLP instructions. Great care must be taken to ensure that all restoration of register values and PC addresses is carried out in exact reverse order from that in which they were saved. If not, a stacking error will result and the computer will attempt to continue program execution at an erroneous address. In the vast majority of cases this will cause a system crash.

You must also be aware of the highest number of bytes that your program will need to save on stack at any one time. The 6502 stack will accommodate only 256 bytes – that is, 128 addresses. After that the stack pointer is decreased from $00 to $FF by a 'wraparound' decrement and once again indexes the higher end of the stack page. Pushing any more addresses or register values will cause previously stacked values to be overwritten. In Chapter 2 we give routines which provide you with a 'user stack'. This may be located in any part of RAM and used for storing variables. The 6502 hardware stack can then be used solely for return addresses and very temporary storage of register values.

Your computer

Most of the software in this book will work on any 6502-based computer. There are, however, certain facts which you must know or find out about your computer before you can begin to use even the simplest machine code routine.

(1) You must know the addresses of RAM (Random Access Memory – memory you can write to and read from) available for use as program storage, data storage and workspace. In high level language programming (e.g. BASIC), the system deals with all storage addresses but in machine code programming you have to

decide where everything goes. One area that is certain to be available is $0000 to $00FF known as *page zero*. This is always used for the storage of system variables because of the special 'zero page' addressing modes.

(2) You must be able to display the present contents of any RAM or ROM (Read Only Memory – unchangeable memory used for operating systems which need to be there when the computer is switched on), and be able to alter RAM contents.

(3) When your machine code program is in place you must know how to cause your computer to execute that program by jumping to the address at which the program starts. It is also useful to know what address to jump to at the end of your program so that the computer system again takes control waiting for your next command.

Some computer systems include a *monitor* which typically will let you see and alter the contents of memory locations, jump to a specified address, copy from one area of memory to another and copy memory to and from tape or disk. Most monitors allow you to use the 'return from subroutine' instruction (RTS) at the end of your program to get back to the monitor. Some expect you to use the software interrupt instruction (BRK). A very few require you to jump (JMP) to a specified address within the monitor.

Better monitors will allow you to set *breakpoints* which stop a program at a specified address. The monitor then displays all register contents, giving you the chance to change them, before continuing execution on command. They may also *single-step* – execute one instruction at a time, displaying registers between the steps. This is useful in testing new programs.

If your built-in software does not have a machine code monitor, BASIC will let you examine and change memory through the use of PEEK and POKE. It should also have a USR or EXEC function to pass control to machine code subroutines.

There are a few other facts which you must know about your computer before you can use all the routines in this book. Most computers use ASCII codes for the alphanumeric characters that can be displayed. Some do not, and if your computer is one of these then you will have to find out what codes are used. Any character codes in this book are from the standard ASCII set (see Appendix C) and may have to be altered to suit your particular system.

The display routines in this book (Chapters 5 to 8) are written for the system known as the *memory-mapped display*. This is the most common method of putting characters on the screen and uses a dedicated area of RAM where each address corresponds to a screen character position. To use the display routines you will have to know the start address of this area of RAM, the number of characters displayed on a line and the difference between the memory addresses of equivalent character positions in adjacent lines. The latter value is not always the same as the number of characters in a line. If your computer uses some other display system, the display routines we give will have to be changed to fit your system. This subject is dealt with at greater depth in Chapter 5.

Since we include routines to check and deal with keyboard input, you will need a routine to scan the keyboard and, if a key is pressed, return with the correct character code. Such a routine is entirely dependent on the hardware design of your computer and we cannot supply anything that is of general use. Your monitor, BASIC interpreter or other system software will have a routine to do this task and you must know the address at which it can be called.

Our system standards demand that the input character code should be returned in the Accumulator and that no other registers or flags are affected. On no input, A should be returned with a value of zero. If the keyboard input routine in your computer does not meet these standards you will have to write an *interface* routine – one which sorts out the difference between two systems at the point where they meet.

The BBC Microcomputer has a particularly awkward keyboard scan routine, INKEY at $FFF4. At entry, A must contain the value $81, and X and Y a time limit to wait for a key press. On exit, if a key has been pressed, the ASCII code is in X, Y is zero and the Carry flag is reset. If no key is pressed, Y = $FF and C = 1. The following code, GETCH, interfaces between INKEY and our system.

```
GETCH:  PHP              ;save P, A, X and Y  08
        PHA              ;on stack.           48
        TXA              ;                    8A
        PHA              ;                    48
        TYA              ;                    98
        PHA              ;                    48
        LDY   #0         ;initialise          A0  00
        LDX   #0         ;registers for       A2  00
        LDA   #$81       ;INKEY needs and     A9  81
        JSR   INKEY      ;go seek input.      20  F4  FF
        LDA   #0         ;A = 0 if no input so A9 00
```

```
            BCS   GSTCH    ;skip if none, else      B0   01
            TXA            ;character code in A. 8A
GSTCH:      TSX            ;index stack by X        BA
            STA   $0103,X  ;and replace stacked 9D  03   01
            PLA            ;A by 0 or code.Then 68
            TAY            ;restore Y, X,           A8
            PLA            ;new A and P             68
            TAX            ;from stack,             AA
            PLA            ;                        68
            PLP            ;                        28
            RTS            ;and return.             60
```

Documentation of routines in this book

Our code is preceded by standard information helpful to its use. *Length* refers to the number of bytes. *Stack* refers to the total number of stack locations needed by the routine and any subroutines that it calls; it does not include the two bytes of stack taken when the routine is called. Each line of code is divided into four *fields*: a label field (used only where necessary), the mnemonic field, comment preceded by a semicolon, and the machine code instruction (one to three bytes long) in hexadecimal.

Chapter Two
Instruction Set Boosters

The 6500 family of processors has a comparatively small number of instructions. This makes it easier to become familiar with those instructions that are available. It also causes the same group of instructions to be used over and over again to carry out some more powerful function than is provided directly. This chapter is about the lowest level of such functions. It gives some useful groups of instructions, in short, simple subroutines, that will often be needed by higher level routines.

To cover all the routines in this book, 64 bytes of page zero memory will be used. The full mapping of these 64 bytes is given in the next chapter. For the utility routines in this chapter only the first eight page zero bytes are needed. These are:

00	USPL	User stack	lo
01	USPH	pointer.	hi
02	TMPL	Temporary storage	lo
03	TMPH	of return address.	hi
04	TMPA	Register A storage.	
05	TMPP	Register P storage.	
06	TMPY	Register Y storage.	
07	TMPX	Register X storage.	

For the purposes of this book, the 64 bytes of reserved page zero memory are numbered in hexadecimal 00 to 3F. You might have to place them in different page zero locations if locations 00 to 3F are used by your machine's system software which you want to remain operative at the same time as these routines.

In addition to the 6502 stack pointer allowing the use of a stack in page 1 of memory (locations $0100 to $01FF) we are providing routines to use a stack of any size, anywhere in memory you choose to place it. The highest address of this user stack has to be put by you in the first reserved page zero locations, USPL-H, with the low order byte of the address first.

The TMP storage in reserved page zero memory is used by the utility routines to store the return address and the registers. Utility routines, except for STTMP, LDTMP and PARAM, operate on two single-byte parameters, P1 and P2, following the jump instruction, so the format for calling them is:

```
JSR    name      20   lo   hi
EQB    $P1,$P2   P1   P2
```

Having the return address in TMPL-H is handy for addressing the parameters when picking them up in order to put them in the processor's registers. It simplifies coding to have the registers saved in page zero, where they can either be altered to return new values or left undisturbed and can also be accessed in any order.

TMP store is considered available for any utility routine to use and overwrite. Any interrupt routine which might use a utility routine calling STTMP would, therefore, have first to save TMP store and exit with it unchanged.

The first thing, then, is to have a routine that will put the contents of the registers into the page zero memory reserved for them and put the contents of the page zero locations back into the registers, when required:

STTMP and LDTMP – Save and recover registers from page zero
Subroutines – None.
Length – 21.
Stack – When entered at STTMP: 1. When entered at LDTMP: 1.
   When entered at LDTMP+3: minus 1.
Input – None.
Output – The registers have been stored or recovered as required.
Registers changed – None.
Method – Instructions up to LDTMP store the registers in the page
   zero locations reserved for them but can possibly have altered the
   A register (to what was initially in the P register) and the sign and
   zero flags of the P register (as a result of the PLA instruction).
   Instructions from LDTMP restore to all registers the values
   previously stored in page zero. When the routine is entered at
   STTMP all the code is executed, in order that, after being stored,
   the registers are unchanged on exit. When the routine is entered at
   LDTMP the registers are simply restored. Entry at LDTMP+3
   restores only the A, X and Y registers from TMP and takes P from

the processor's stack. This allows a calling routine to pass on information in the P register.

STTMP:	STA	TMPA	;store accumulator,	85	04
	STX	TMPX	;X register and Y	86	07
	STY	TMPY	;register in page z.	84	06
	PHP		;push P onto stack,	08	
	PLA		;pull it back into A	68	
	STA	TMPP	;and store in page z.	85	05
LDTMP:	LDA	TMPP	;get original P in	A5	05
	PHA		;A to stack it.	48	
	LDA	TMPA	;recover A,	A5	04
	LDX	TMPX	;X and	A6	07
	LDY	TMPY	;Y.	A4	06
	PLP		;recover original P	28	
	RTS		;and return.	60	

Since the later utility routines are going to operate on parameters embedded in the code, we now need a routine (1) to take up those parameters into the processor's registers and (2) to update the address on the stack used to return to the code calling a routine with parameters, so that the parameters are skipped on exit and not executed as code. We call this routine PARAM and, to help understanding of it, here is an example, illustrated with code and stack addresses, of the position at the fifth instruction of PARAM, assuming an empty stack to start with.

CODE
Hex address

1656		—				
1657	JSR	PSHZM	20	3B	12
165A	EQB	$P1,$P2	nn	nn	
165C		—-				
123B PSHZM:	JSR	PARAM	20	15	12
		—				
	RTS		60		
1215 PARAM:	JSR	STTMP			
1218	PHP				
1219	CLD				
121A	CLC				

STACK

| 01FF | 16 | unadjusted return address −1 from | hi |
| 01FE | 59 | PSHZM to main code. | lo |

01FD	12	return address −1 from PARAM	hi
01FC	3D	to code in PSHZM.	lo
01FB		contents of the P register.	
01FA			stack pointer = $FA

The contents of the P register, at stack address $01FB, have, at this stage, overwritten the return address from STTMP to the code in PARAM. The 8-bit stack pointer contains $FA, the high order byte $01 of the stack address being assumed. The TSX instruction in PARAM transfers the stack pointer value $FA to the X register so that the LDA $0104,X instruction loads the byte at address $0104 + $FA = &01FE. The rest is straightforward enough.

PARAM – Get two embedded parameters
Subroutines – STTMP.
Length – 38.
Stack – 3.
Input – None.
Output – X = Parameter 1. A and Y = Parameter 2. Registers are saved in TMP. TMPL-H holds the address of the byte preceding Parameter 1. The return address on the stack is incremented by 2 to skip the parameters.
Registers changed – A, X and Y.
Method – The routine relies on the fact that the 6502 processor stack is fixed in page 1 of memory and that 5 bytes have been added to the stack from the call by the routine with parameters. Using the stack pointer as an index, it is possible to pick up the return address from the routine with embedded parameters, adjust it on the stack to skip the parameters on exit and use it in TMPH-L to address the parameters.

PARAM:	JSR	STTMP	;save regs. in pz.	20	lo	hi
	PHP		;save D & C status.	08		
	CLD		;clear decimal mode	D8		
	CLC		;& carry for bin. add.	18		
	TSX		;indexing with	BA		
	LDA	$0104,X	;stack pointer get	BD	04	01
	STA	TMPL	;return address −1	85	02	
	ADC	#2	;into page zero	69	02	
	STA	$0104,X	;TMPH-L as address	9D	04	01
	LDA	$0105,X	;of parameters. Adjust	BD	05	01
	STA	TMPH	;return address on	85	03	
	ADC	#0	;stack past the	69	00	
	STA	$0105,X	;two parameters.	9D	05	01

```
LDY   #1           ;index first param.   A0   01
LDA   (TMPL),Y     ;get it into X        B1   02
TAX                ;via A.               AA
INY                ;index next.          C8
LDA   (TMPL),Y     ;get into A and       B1   02
TAY                ;into Y via A.        A8
PLP                ;restore flags        28
RTS                ;and return.          60
```

The first utility routines that operate on parameters embedded in the code come next. PSHZM pushes any page zero bytes selected from a block of eight onto the user stack and PULZM pulls bytes from the user stack back into page zero memory, both adjusting the user stack pointer USPL-H.

The first parameter following the JSR instruction gives the lowest address of the 8-byte block and the setting of bits in the second parameter determines which page zero bytes are to be pushed or pulled. The most significant (left-most) bit of parameter 2 refers to the page zero byte at parameter 1 address $+ 7$ and the least significant bit, to the page zero byte at parameter 1 address $+ 0$. For example:

```
JSR   PSHZM
EQB   $08,$FF
```

would push the eight bytes at $0F to $08, in that order. Having parameter 2 = $3F would push the six bytes at $0D to $08 and having parameter 2 = $F2 would push the five bytes at $0F to $0C and $09. A parameter address at $FE would cause wraparound, i.e. the routine would operate on the 8-byte block $FE to $05.

PSHZM – Push up to eight page zero bytes, selected from an 8-byte block, onto the user stack

Subroutines – PARAM, STTMP, LDTMP.

Length – 28.

Stack – 5. *User Stack* – up to 8, depending on parameter 2.

Input – Parameter 1 = base address of 8-byte block of page zero memory. Parameter 2 = byte select mask (bit set = push). The most significant bit of the mask corresponds to the highest addressed byte of memory.

Output – Selected bytes from page zero are stored on the user stack. The user stack pointer, USPL-H, is decremented accordingly.

Registers changed – None.

Method – The routine uses parameters 1 and 2, put into X and Y respectively by PARAM. The highest addressed page zero byte is dealt with first by (1) shifting the bit mask, one bit at a time, left from A, and (2) when the bit is set, loading the page zero byte addressed by 7 + the successively decreasing 8-byte block address. After any byte is stored on the user stack, its stack pointer is decreased by one. The operation ends as soon as there are no remaining byte mask bits set, without necessarily having tested all 8 bits individually.

Since PSHZM first calls PARAM, which calls STTMP, which puts all the registers in TMP store, registers can be pushed onto the user stack by making parameter 2 address TMP store.

PSHZM:	JSR	PARAM	;save rgs & get parms.	20	lo	hi
	LDY	#0	;zero index user SP.	A0	00	
PHL:	ASL	A	;shift mask bit out.	0A		
	PHA		;save mask. If bit set	48		
	BCC	PHLT	;get corresponding pz	90	0C	
	LDA	$07,X	;byte and store it in	B5	07	
	STA	(USPL),Y	;location whose addr	91	00	
	LDA	USPL	;given at pz USPL-H	A5	00	
	BNE	PHD	;(user stack pointer).	D0	02	
	DEC	USPH	;decrement user	C6	01	
PHD:	DEC	USPL	;stack pointer.	C6	00	
PHLT:	DEX		;index next pz byte.	CA		
	PLA		;restore mask, repeat	68		
	BNE	PHL	;if any set bits left.	D0	EC	
	JMP	LDTMP	;get regs. from pz.	4C	lo	hi

PULZM – Pull up to eight bytes from the user stack back into selected locations of an 8-byte block
Subroutines – PARAM, STTMP, LDTMP.
Length – 26.
Stack – 5. *User Stack* – Up to minus 8, depending on parameter 2.
Input – Parameter 1 = base address of an 8-byte block of page zero memory. Parameter 2 = byte select mask (bit set = pull). The least significant bit of the mask corresponds to the lowest addressed byte of memory.
Output – Bytes from the user stack are moved to selected page zero locations. The user stack is incremented accordingly.
Registers changed – None, unless PULZM addresses TMPA,P,Y or X, when registers would be pulled from the user stack.
Method – The routine uses parameters 1 and 2, put into X and A respectively by PARAM. The lowest addressed page zero byte is

dealt with first by (1) shifting the byte select mask, one bit at a time, right from A and (2) when the bit is set, storing the byte taken from the user stack into the page zero location addressed by 0 + the successively increasing 8-byte block base address. The stack pointer is increased by 1, before any byte is taken from the user stack. The operation ends as soon as there are no remaining byte mask bits set, without necessarily having tested all eight bits individually.

Registers that have previously been pushed onto the user stack can be restored by making parameter 2 address TMP store. In this case, the registers from the user stack will be put into TMP store, from where they will be placed in the processor's registers on exit via LDTMP.

PULZM:	JSR	PARAM	;save regs, get params.	20	lo	hi
	LDY	#0	;index to user SP.	A0	00	
PLL:	LSR	A	;shift mask bit out.	4A		
	PHA		;save mask.	48		
	BCC	PLLT	;if bit is set	90	0A	
	INC	USPL	;increment user	E6	00	
	BNE	PLI	;stack pointer and	D0	02	
	INC	USPH	;pull byte to	E6	01	
PLI:	LDA	(USPL),Y	;corresponding	B1	00	
	STA	$00,X	;page zero byte.	95	00	
PLLT:	INX		;index next pz byte.	E8		
	PLA		;restore mask. Repeat	68		
	BNE	PLL	;if any set bit left.	D0	EE	
	JMP	LDTMP	;get regs. from pz.	4C	lo	hi

The next four utilities move 2-byte words about in memory, as needed often by other routines. Like PSHZM and PULZM, they all save registers in TMP store, returning via LDTMP to recover them. No special explanation of method is needed for these simple routines.

LDZE – Transfer a 2-byte word to page zero from anywhere in memory outside page zero
Subroutines – PARAM, STTMP, LDTMP.
Length – 28.
Stack – 5.
Input – Parameter 1 = Address of the first byte of the page zero destination. Parameter 2 = Address of the first byte of a page zero word holding the address (lo hi) of the extended memory source.

Output – The word in memory outside page zero is copied into the page zero locations specified.

Registers changed – None.

LDZE:	JSR	PARAM	;save regs. get params.	20	lo	hi
	LDA	$0000,Y	;move memory pointer	B9	00	00
	STA	TMPL	;to TMP store for	85	02	
	INY		;post-indexed	C8		
	LDA	$0000,Y	;indirect	B9	00	00
	STA	TMPH	;addressing.	85	03	
	LDY	#0	;move first	A0	00	
	LDA	(TMPL),Y	;byte to	B1	02	
	STA	$00,X	;page zero.	95	00	
	INY		;move second	C8		
	LDA	(TMPL),Y	;byte to	B1	02	
	STA	$01,X	;page zero.	95	01	
	JMP	LDTMP	;get regs. from pz.	4C	lo	hi

STZE – Transfer a 2-byte word from page zero to anywhere in memory outside page zero

Subroutines – PARAM, STTMP, LDTMP.

Length – 28.

Stack – 5.

Input – Parameter 1 = Address of the first byte of the page zero source. Parameter 2 = Address of the first byte of the page zero word holding the address (lo hi) of the extended memory destination.

Output – The word in page zero is copied to the address specified outside page zero.

Registers changed – None.

STZE:	JSR	PARAM	;save regs. get params.	20	lo	hi
	LDA	$0000,Y	;move memory pointer	B9	00	00
	STA	TMPL	;to TMP store for	85	02	
	INY		;post-indexed	C8		
	LDA	$0000,Y	;indirect	B9	00	00
	STA	TMPH	;addressing.	85	03	
	LDY	#0	;move first byte	A0	00	
	LDA	$00,X	;from page zero to	B5	00	
	STA	(TMPL),Y	;extended area RAM.	91	02	
	INY		;move second byte	C8		
	LDA	#01,X	;from page zero to	B5	01	
	STA	(TMPL),Y	;extended area RAM.	91	02	
	JMP	LDTMP	;get regs. from pz.	4C	lo	hi

EXGZZ – Exchange two page zero words
Subroutines – PARAM, STTMP, LDTMP.
Length – 31.
Stack – 5.
Input – Parameter 1 = Address of the first byte of a page zero word.
  Parameter 2 = Address of the first byte of another page zero
  word.
Output – The positions of the two page zero words are reversed.
Registers changed – None.

EXGZZ:	JSR	PARAM	;save regs. get params.	20	lo	hi
	LDA	$00,X	;load P1 first byte.	B5	00	
	PHA		;put it on 6502 stack.	48		
	LDA	$0000,Y	;load P2 first byte.	B9	00	00
	STA	$00,X	;put it in P1 place.	95	00	
	PLA		;recover P1 1st byte.	68		
	STA	$0000,Y	;put it in P2 place.	99	00	00
	INY		;point to next byte.	C8		
	LDA	$01,X	;load P1 2nd byte.	B5	01	
	PHA		;put it on 6502 stack.	48		
	LDA	$0000,Y	;load P2 2nd byte.	B9	00	00
	STA	$01,X	;put it in P1 place.	95	01	
	PLA		;recover P1 2nd byte.	68		
	STA	$0000,Y	;put it in P2 place.	99	00	00
	JMP	LDTMP	;get regs. from pz.	4C	lo	hi

TFRZZ – Transfer a 2-byte word from one page zero location to another
Subroutines – PARAM, STTMP, LDTMP.
Length – 17.
Stack – 5.
Input – Parameter 1 = Address of the first byte of the page zero word
  to be transferred. Parameter 2 = Address of the first byte of the
  page zero destination.
Output – The word is copied from the P1 address to the P2 address.
Registers changed – None.

TFRZZ:	JSR	PARAM	;save regs. get params.	20	lo	hi
	LDA	$00,X	;get P1 first byte	B5	00	
	STA	$0000,Y	;to P2 first byte.	99	00	00
	INY		;point to next byte.	C8		
	LDA	$01,X	;get P1 second byte	B5	01	
	STA	$0000,Y	;to P2 second byte.	99	00	00
	JMP	LDTMP	;get regs. from pz.	4C	lo	hi

Simple addition and subtraction, with any carry or borrow previously generated, comes next. The first two of these utilities add or subtract a 1-byte to a 2-byte value and the second two add or subtract 2 2-byte values. 2-byte values are held with the least significant byte preceding the most significant. When doing addition, the carry flag set (= 1) denotes that a carry has to be added in, whilst, in subtraction, the carry flag reset (= 0) denotes that a borrow has to be taken off. Note that these four utilities save registers in TMP store but return via LDTMP+3, so that the flags are not recovered from TMP but from the processor stack, where the add and subtract routines place them. In this way the flags' status, resulting from the arithmetic, is passed on.

ADCZI – Add with carry an 8-bit unsigned value to a word in page zero
Subroutines – PARAM, STTMP, LDTMP.
Length – 21.
Stack – 5.
Input – Parameter 1 = Address of the first byte of a word in page zero holding a binary value (lo hi). Parameter 2 = An 8-bit unsigned value.
Output – The 8-bit value + any carry has been added to the page zero word.
Registers changed – P.

ADCZI:	JSR	PARAM	;save regs. get params.	20	lo	hi
	LDA	$00,X	;get first pz byte.	B5	00	
	STY	$00,X	;store P2 value. Add	94	00	
	ADC	$00,X	;P2 to A. Result to	75	00	
	STA	$00,X	;first page zero byte.	95	00	
	LDA	$01,X	;get 2nd pz byte. Add	B5	01	
	ADC	#0	;zero + any carry.	69	00	
	STA	$01,X	;Result to 2nd pz.	95	01	
	PHP		;stack result flags	08		
	JMP	LDTMP+3	;for return in P.	4C	lo	hi

SBCZI – Subtract with borrow 8-bit unsigned value from page zero word
Subroutines – PARAM, STTMP, LDTMP.
Length – 21.
Stack – 5.
Input – Parameter 1 = Address of the first byte of a word in page zero holding a binary value (lo hi). Parameter 2 = An 8-bit unsigned value.

Output – The 8-bit value and any borrow has been taken from the
page zero word.
Registers changed – P.

SBCZI:	JSR	PARAM	;save regs. get params.	20	lo	hi
	LDA	$00,X	;get first pz byte.	B5	00	
	STY	$00,X	;store P2 value.take	94	00	
	SBC	$00,X	;P2 from 1st pz value.	F5	00	
	STA	$00,X	;put result in 1st pz.	95	00	
	LDA	$01,X	;get 2nd pz byte.	B5	01	
	SBC	#0	;subt. 0 & any borrow.	E9	00	
	STA	$01,X	;put result in 2nd pz.	95	01	
	PHP		;stack results flags.	08		
	JMP	LDTMP+3	;for return in P.	4C	lo	hi

ADCZZ – Add with carry two page zero words

Subroutines – PARAM, STTMP, LDTMP.

Length – 22.

Stack – 5.

Input – Parameter 1 = Address of the first byte of a 2-byte binary
value (lo hi) in page zero. Parameter 2 = Address of the first byte
of another binary word (lo hi) in page zero.

Output – The result of the addition is in the page zero word
addressed by P1.

Registers changed – P.

Method – With the P1 address in X and the P2 address in Y, the code
shows that a 1-byte page zero address (zero in this case) may be
indexed by X, but not by Y. The only exceptions to this are the
LDX and STX instructions, where a 1-byte page zero location can
be indexed by Y.

ADCZZ:	JSR	PARAM	;save regs.get params.	20	lo	hi
	LDA	$00,X	;get first P1 byte.	B5	00	
	ADC	$0000,Y	;add first P2 byte.	79	00	00
	STA	$00,X	;result back to P1.	95	00	
	INY		;repeat	C8		
	LDA	$01,X	;for second	B5	01	
	ADC	$0000,Y	;P1 and P2	79	00	00
	STA	$01,X	;bytes.	95	01	
	PHP		;stack result flags	08		
	JMP	LDTMP+3	;for return in P.	4C	lo	hi

SBCZZ – Subtract, with any borrow, two page zero words

Subroutines – PARAM, STTMP, LDTMP.

Length – 22.

Stack – 5.

Input – Parameter 1 = Address of the first byte of a 2-byte binary value (lo hi) in page zero. Parameter 2 = Address of the first byte of another binary word in page zero.

Output – The result of the subtraction (lo hi) is in the binary word addressed by P1.

Registers changed – P.

SBCZZ:	JSR	PARAM	;save regs.get params.	20	lo	hi
	LDA	$00,X	;get first P1 byte.	B5	00	
	SBC	$0000,Y	;subtract 1st P2 byte.	F9	00	00
	STA	$00,X	;result back to P1.	95	00	
	INY		;repeat	C8		
	LDA	$01,X	;for second	B5	01	
	SBC	$0000,Y	;P1 and P2	F9	00	00
	STA	$01,X	;bytes.	95	01	
	PHP		;stack result flags	08		
	JMP	LDTMP+3	;for return in P.	4C	lo	hi

The last utility is a multiple choice one. On a 2-byte word in page zero, the address of the first word of which is in parameter 1, it does one of eight things – depending on the value (0 to 7) of the least significant 3 bits of parameter 2. The binary selection of the action to be performed is of particular interest. Figure 2.1 shows how any of the eight operations is selected in a maximum of three tests.

MUG – Multiple choice utility group

Subroutines – PARAM, STTMP, LDTMP.

Length – 126.

Stack – 5.

Input – Parameter 1 = Address of the first byte of a 2-byte word in page zero. The least significant 3 bits of Parameter 2 hold the action select code: 0 = CLR: zeroise P1 word. 1 = EXG: exchange bytes of P1 word. 2 = CPL: 1's (9's) complement P1 word. 3 = MUL: multiply the two bytes giving the result (lo hi) at P1. 4 = SEX: extend the sign of the first P1 byte through the other byte, so that the single byte value becomes a double-byte value. 5 = SRT: if the second P1 byte is less than the first, exchange the bytes, so that the first of the two bytes always has the lower value. 6 = NEG: 2's (10's) complement the (lo hi) P1 word. 7 = DIV: divide the second P1 byte by the first with the result in the first and the remainder in the second byte.

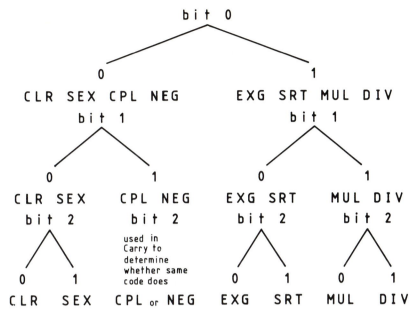

Fig. 2.1. Binary selection in MUG.

Output – As specified by the action select code.

Registers changed – In CPL, SEX, SRT and NEG flags might be changed. Otherwise all registers are unchanged.

Method – At label CN, the same code 1's or 2's complements according to whether the carry is reset or set. The 8-bit multiplication/division is done by shifting and adding/subtracting.

MUG:	JSR	PARAM	;save regs.get params.	20	lo	hi
	AND	#%00000111	;clear non-code bits.	29	07	
	LSR	A	;EXG SRT MUL DIV or	4A		
	BCS	ESMD	;CLR SEX CPL NEG.	B0	28	
CSCN:	LSR	A	;select CPL NEG	4A		
	BCS	CN	;or CLR SEX.	B0	16	
CS:	LSR	A	;select Sign EXtend	4A		
	BCS	SEX	;or CLeaR.	B0	07	
CLR:	STA	$00,X	;shifts cleared A so	95	00	
	STA	$01,X	;A clears pz lo hi.	95	01	
	JMP	LDTMP	;return with pz regs.	4C	lo	hi
SEX:	LDY	$00,X	;test 1st byte sign	B4	00	
	BPL	SEXH	;changing A = $00 to	10	02	
	ORA	#$FF	;A=$FF if negative.	09	FF	
SEXH:	STA	$01,X	;store 2nd byte and	95	01	
	PHP		;stack sign flag	08		

	JMP	LDTMP+3	;for return in P.	4C	lo	hi
CN:	LSR	A	;bit 2 used in SBC	4A		
	SBC	$00,X	;to effect 1's comp-	F5	00	
	STA	$00,X	;lement (CPL) if 0,	95	00	
	LDA	#0	;else 2's	A9	00	
	SBC	$01,X	;complement (NEG)	F5	01	
	STA	$01,X	;if 1.	95	01	
	PHP		;stack result flags	08		
	JMP	LDTMP+3	;for return in P.	4C	lo	hi
ESMD:	LSR	A	;select MUL DIV	4A		
	BCS	MD	;or EXG SRT.	B0	1E	
ES:	LSR	A	;select SoRT	4A		
	LDA	$01,X	;(after getting hi &	B5	01	
	LDY	$00,X	;lo bytes of pz)	B4	00	
	BCS	SRT	;or EXchanGe by	B0	07	
EXG:	STA	$00,X	;putting back in	95	00	
	STY	$01,X	;reverse order.	94	01	
	JMP	LDTMP	;return with pz regs.	4C	lo	hi
SRT:	CMP	$00,X	;exchange only if	D5	00	
	BCS	SRTF	;2nd byte < 1st byte	B0	04	
	STA	$00,X	;by putting back in	95	00	
	STY	$01,X	;reverse order.	94	01	
SRTF:	PHP		;complement carry so	08		
	PLA		;it is set only if	68		
	EOR	#%00000001	;exchange occurred.	49	01	
	PHA		;stack result flags	48		
	JMP	LDTMP+3	;for return in P.	4C	lo	hi
MD:	LDY	#8	;load 8-bit counter.	A0	08	
	CLD		;set for binary arith.	D8		
	LSR	A	;select DIVision	4A		
	BCS	DIV	;or MULtiplication.	B0	14	
MUL:	ASL	A	;shift part product.	0A		
	ROL	$01,X	;shift multiplier.	36	01	
	BCC	MULT	;skip if no add at	90	07	
	CLC		;this place, else add	18		
	ADC	$00,X	;multiplicand to	75	00	
	BCC	MULT	;part product with	90	02	
	INC	$01,X	;carry to 8-bit ovflw.	F6	01	
MULT:	DEY		;repeat for 8 bits	88		
	BNE	MUL	;of multiplier	D0	F1	
	STA	$00,X	;lo byte rslt to pz.	95	00	
	JMP	LDTMP	;return with pz regs.	4C	lo	hi
DIV:	ASL	$01,X	;shift dividend into	16	01	
	ROL	A	;remainder, test if	2A		
	CMP	$00,X	;divisor subtracts.	D5	00	

	BCC	DIVT	;subtract if it will	90	04	
	SBC	$00,X	;& set part quotient	F5	00	
	INC	$01,X	;place bit.	F6	01	
DIVT:	DEY		;repeat for 8 bits	88		
	BNE	DIV	;of dividend.	D0	F2	
	STA	$00,X	;remainder to pz.	95	00	
	JMP	LDTMP	;return with pz regs.	4C	lo	hi

Three of the routines in this chapter, **PSHZM**, **PULZM** and **MUG**, use instructions to branch by the value given in the second byte of the instruction, which is known as the displacement. This can be either negative (to branch backwards) or positive (to branch forwards). Anybody new to machine code and not using an assembler, has to get used to the fact that the displacement is calculated from the first byte after the end of the branch instruction. An assembler, which allows you to show a label to be branched to, calculates these displacements for you.

Look at the fourth instruction in MUG, BCS ESMD (B0 28). The displacement $28, or decimal 40, is calculated from the byte containing $4A and takes you to another byte containing $4A, where the label ESMD is. Near the end of the routine, one down from the label MULT, is the instruction BNE MUL (D0 F1). The displacement $F1, or decimal −15, calculated from the byte containing $95, takes you to the byte containing $0A, where the label MUL is.

Chapter Three
Organising for Character Display

Programming a major application in machine code is a very different matter from writing a single routine to perform some limited, easily defined task. For one thing, there is more data to be considered than can conveniently be passed in the few registers the 6502 processor has. To remedy this we reserve space in page zero for four 16-bit user registers. These should be treated in the same way as the processor's registers by being saved before use so that they can be returned unchanged after use. You have seen how calls to PSHZM and PULZM can do this. We also saw the advantages of storing the 6502 registers in page zero rather than on the processor's stack. Other locations in page zero ought to be reserved, where information most commonly needed throughout an application will always be found by whatever routine needs it.

There is another advantage in having these reserved memory areas. They offer more scope for writing routines that can be made to do different things simply by altering the information in memory, rather than by altering any code. This should become clear as you read on.

For ease and economy of addressing it, all this common information, or addresses pointing to it, is in page zero. It requires 64 bytes laid out as follows, though perhaps with a different base address to suit your system:

00	USPL	lo	{ user stack	**The User Stack**
01	USPH	hi	{ pointer.	

02	TMPL	lo	{ general	**Temporary storage**
03	TMPH	hi	{ storage.	
04	TMPA		register A storage	
05	TMPP		register P storage	
06	TMPY		register Y storage.	
07	TMPX		register X storage.	

08	UAL	lo	{user	**The 16-bit user 'registers'**
09	UAH	hi	register A.	
0A	UBL	lo	{user	
0B	UBH	hi	register B.	
0C	UCL	lo	{user	
0D	UCH	hi	register C.	
0E	UDL	lo	{user	
0F	UDH	hi	register D.	

| 10 | KCH | | keyed input chr. | **Character string data** |
| 11 | PCH | | character to print. | |

| 12 | DELH | | 1/100 sec delay factor. | **Delay information** |
| 13 | DELN | | no. of 1/100 secs delay. | |

14	PRAL	lo	{prompt message	**Prompt information**
15	PRAH	hi	string address.	
16	PRT		index to last character.	
17	PRF		character index.	

18	BYTL	lo	{address of	**Extended memory addresses**
19	BYTH	hi	byte storage.	**of storage**
1A	WRDL	lo	{address of	
1B	WRDH	hi	word storage.	
1C	STRL	lo	{address of	
1E	STRH	hi	character strings.	
1E	ARRL	lo	{address of two-	
1F	ARRH	hi	dimensional arrays.	
20	DAPL	lo	{address of display	
21	DAPH	hi	area parameter tables.	

22	CCN		cursor character index.	**Display information**
23	CLN		cursor line index.	
24	CCDL	lo	{cursor character	
25	CCDH	hi	byte displacement.	
26	CLDL	lo	{cursor line	
27	CLDH	hi	byte displacement.	

28	DHL	lo	{the home	**The current display area**
29	DHH	hi	address.	
2A	DCN		character high index.	

2B	DLN		line high index.	
2C	DCDL	lo	⎰ single character	
2D	DCDH	hi	⎱ byte difference.	
2E	DLDL	lo	⎰ single line	
2F	DLDH	hi	⎱ byte difference.	

30	GOL	lo	⎰ graphics origin	**Graphics information**
31	GOH	hi	⎱ address.	
32	GXN		*x* pixels high index.	
33	GYN		*y* pixels high index.	
34	PLTX		plot *x* coordinate.	
35	PLTY		plot *y* coordinate.	
36	DRWX		draw *x* coordinate.	
37	DRWY		draw *y* coordinate.	
38	PLTM		plot mode.	
39	PLTR		plot result.	
3A	TLTX		translation vector *x*.	
3B	TLTY		translation vector *y*.	
3C	TFMC		transformation code.	

3D	AMO	operator storage.	**Calculator use.**
3E	AMW	workspace.	
3F	AML	digit length.	

Display area information

This provides all we need to know when displaying characters on a memory mapped screen. It is in two parts; the current display area, which defines the screen area in use at any one time and the display information, which keeps track of the cursor as it is moved about the current display area.

In the current display area, the home address can be that of any character position on the screen because the direction of displaying from this address is determined by the character and line byte differences. Horizontal movement is to the right of the home address when the character byte difference is positive and to the left when it is negative. Vertical movement is downwards from the home address when the line byte difference is positive and upwards when it is negative.

A standard 40 col × 25 line display, with the home address at the top left-hand corner, would have a character byte difference of $01 and line difference of $28. These could be doubled to skip alternate columns and rows or the line difference can be set to accommodate those video display maps where a row does not start at an address one more than the end of the previous row but has a margin between rows. Characters and lines are indexed from 0 so, on our standard screen, the character high index would be $27 and the line high index $18. These indices are used to mark the end of a line and screen respectively.

In display information, the cursor character and line indices are initially set at 0 and show the number of characters displayed on the current line or the number of lines displayed on the screen. The character and line byte displacements are used by the display routines to accumulate the number of bytes of the video display taken by each cursor movement. The character byte displacement holds the value of the cursor character index multiplied by the single character byte difference. The line byte displacement holds the value of the cursor line index multiplied by the single line byte difference. The current cursor address is therefore the home address + the line byte displacement + the character byte displacement. The cursor is home when all the display information is at zero. Here is a little routine to home the cursor:

HOME – Home cursor to line 0, character 0
Subroutines – STTMP, LDTMP.
Stack – 3.
Input – None.
Output – All display information is set to zero.
Registers changed – None.

HOME:	JSR	STTMP	;store regs. in pz.	20	lo	hi
	LDX	#6	;count six bytes.	A2	06	
	LDA	#0	;clear A and use to	A9	00	
HOMEL:	DEX		;clear 6 bytes from	CA		
	STA	CCN,X	;lowest cursor	95	22	
	BNE	HOMEL	;variable.	D0	FB	
	JMP	LDTMP	;recover regs from pz.	4C	lo	hi

To do away with the need to code a new setting of the current display area each time the screen limits are changed, provision is made for an area of RAM to be set aside to hold a number of sets of pre-defined display area parameters, any one of which can be moved into the current display area by a common routine. These parameter sets are referred to by numbers from 0 upwards. The base address of the pre-defined display area parameters must be given (lo hi) in page zero locations DAPL-H. This is the common system routine to move any one of 32 sets of parameters to the current display area.

RDAP – Get any one of 32 sets of parameters into the current display area
Subroutines – HOME, STTMP, LDTMP.
Length – 20.
Stack – 5.
Input – A = the number of the required display area parameter set.
Output – The parameter set is moved to the current display area and the cursor is homed.
Registers changed – None.
Method – To calculate the displacement from the address at DAPL-H, the display area number is multiplied by 8 by three shifts left. This allows for a maximum display area number of 31, as beyond this the most significant bit would be shifted out and lost.

RDAP:	JSR	HOME	;home cursor;save rgs	20	lo	hi
	ASL	A	;in TMP store. DAP	0A		
	ASL	A	;no. × 8 for 8 bytes	0A		
	ASL	A	;in each area set.	0A		
	TAY		;Y indexes DAP sets.	A8		
	LDX	#−8	;X indxs current DA.	A2	F8	
RDAPL:	LDA	(DAPL),Y	;get DAP byte. index	B1	20	
	INY		;next.index current	C8		
	INX		;DA byte and	E8		
	STA	DLDH,X	;set parameter.	95	2F	
	BNE	RDAPL	;repeat for all 8.	D0	F8	
	JMP	LDTMP	;recover pz regs.	4C	lo	hi

Character strings

An area of RAM is reserved for any text to be used in an application and the start address of this area is given in page zero locations STRL-H. The first byte of each character string is an 8-bit unsigned value, which will not be displayed, giving the number of bytes (up to 255) in the remainder of the string. A length byte of zero means that the string consists of only that byte and no text characters. Characters in a string can be any that the computer will display. The strings are referred to by number, from 0 up.

Our system of printing strings prints from the 16-bit address in user register 'A' at page zero UAL-H, indexed by the 8-bit value in UBH until this has reached the 8-bit value in UBL. We have two system routines (STRNG and SBSTR) to get string information into the user registers for either a complete, or part of a previously set up, character string as follows.

STRNG – Get string A information into user registers
Subroutines – TFRZZ, PARAM, STTMP, LDTMP.
Length – 33.
Stack – 5.
Input – A = the number of the character string, whose information is requested.
Output – User register 'A' holds the address of the length byte of the requested string. UBH = 1 (from). UBL = the string length (to).
Registers changed – None.
Method – Starting with the base address of the character string RAM area, the routine adds 1 for the string length byte and the actual string length for each string in the area before the one requested. On the last loop, the X count = 1 and the requested string length is in Y, with these values in UBH and UBL respectively.

STRNG:	JSR	TFRZZ	;str addr to user A	20	lo	hi
	EQB	STRL,UAL	;with regs. in TMP.	1C	08	
	CLD		;ensure binary arith.	D8		
	LDY	#0	;indx lgth byte by Y.	A0	00	
	TAX		;set X as count of	AA		
	INX		;string number + 1.	E8		
STR:	STX	UBH	;"from" = 1 on exit.	86	0B	
	LDA	(UAL),Y	;current string lgth	B1	08	
	STA	UBL	;byte to "to" store.	85	0A	
	DEX		;end if this is the	CA		
	BEQ	STRND	;requested string.	F0	0B	
	SEC		;else,with carry to	38		
	ADC	UAL	;inc past length byte.	65	08	
	STA	UAL	;add length to point-	85	08	
	BCC	STR	;er & index next	90	F0	
	INC	UAH	;string. loop till	E6	09	
	BCS	STR	;wanted string found.	B0	EC	
STRND:	JMP	LDTMP	;restore pz regs.	4C	lo	hi

SBSTR – Get information for string A from characters X to Y into user registers
Subroutines – STRNG,TFRZZ,PARAM,STTMP,LDTMP.

Length – 20.

Stack – 9.

Input – A = number of the string for which information is wanted.
X = 'from' character position. Y = 'to' character position. X = 0
means start from beginning of string; Y = 0 means go to end of
string.

Output – User register 'A' holds the address of the length byte of the
requested string. UBH indexes the 'from' and UBL the 'to'
character.

Registers changed – None.

SBSTR:	JSR	STRNG	;get complete string	20	lo hi
	TXA		;info. If X was 0	8A	
	BEQ	SBSTO	;leave 'from' = 1,	F0	02
	STA	UBH	;else 'from' = X.	85	0B
SBSTO:	TYA		;if Y was 0 leave	98	
	BEQ	SBSND	;'to' = string length	F0	06
	CMP	UBL	;else 'to'=lesser of	C5	0A
	BCS	SBSND	;string length or	B0	02
	STA	UBL	;requested 'to'.	85	0A
SBSND:	JMP	LDTMP	;recover pz regs.	4C	lo hi

Arrays

The start address of an area of RAM reserved for arrays must be
given at page zero locations ARRL-H. The array format allows for
2-dimensional arrays and has a first byte giving the number (1 to
255) of columns and a second byte giving the number (1 to 255) of
rows. The next byte is row 1 col 1, followed by row 1 col 2 and so on.
When an array is used as a list of equal length strings, the first byte
gives the length of the strings and the second, the number of strings.
If either the first or second byte is zero then the array is empty and
consists only of the two information bytes. An array with a first byte
of 1 is, in effect, a one-dimensional array.

When asking a user to choose one of a limited set of responses, it is
useful to have a list of acceptable replies set up against which the
actual reply can be checked. We are going to use one- and two-
dimensional arrays for these lists and two-dimensional arrays to
hold shape tables for the drawing routines. Arrays are referred to by
number from 0 upwards. In our system arrays are used with the
address in user register 'A', the number of columns in page zero

location UBL and the number of rows in UBH. Here is a system routine to set this information up for a nominated array:

ARRAY – Get array A information into user registers

Subroutines – TFRZZ,LDZE,MUG,ADCZZ,PARAM,STTMP, LDTMP.

Length – 42.

Stack – 9.

Input – A = the number of array for which information wanted.

Output – The address of the byte preceding the first element is in user register 'A'. The number of columns is in UBL and the number of rows is in UBH.

Registers changed – None.

Method – TFRZZ moves the address at page zero locations ARRL-H to user register 'A'. LDZE moves column and row information to UBL-H for the array pointed to by user register 'A'. MUG multiplies UBL by UBH with the result in UBL-H. ADCZZ adds the value in UBL-H to user register 'A'.

ARRAY:	JSR	TFRZZ	;move array RAM base	20	lo	hi
	EQB	ARRL,UAL	;address to user 'A'.	1E	08	
	PHP		;save the P and	08		
	PHA		;A registers. Clear	48		
	CLD		;for binary arith.	D8		
ARL:	JSR	LDZE	;move current array	20	lo	hi
	EQB	UBL,UAL	;col/row to user 'B'.	0A	08	
	INC	UAL	;point user 'A'	E6	08	
	BNE	ARLT	;to byte before	D0	02	
	INC	UAH	;first element.	E6	09	
ARLT:	ORA	#0	;action zero flag &	09	00	
	BEQ	ARND	;end if wanted array.	F0	10	
	JSR	MUG	;else rows × cols =	20	lo	hi
	EQB	UBL,$03	;array length.Add to	0A	03	
	SEC		;pointer, carry inc's	38		
	JSR	ADCZZ	;past rows byte, to	20	lo	hi
	EQB	UAL,UBL	;point to next array.	08	0A	
	SEC		;decrement array	38		
	SBC	#1	;number count and	E9	01	
	BCS	ARL	;loop to next array.	B0	E1	
ARND:	PLA		;restore A	68		
	PLP		;and P registers	28		
	RTS		;and return.	60		

Byte and word storage

Two more areas of RAM are reserved for byte storage and 16-bit word storage. The base address of byte storage must be given in page zero locations BYTL-H and the word storage address in WRDL-H. Again, bytes and words are referred to by number, from 0 up. Special routines are hardly needed to write and read bytes to and from storage but we have two system routines to write and read words. Words are written from or read to specified page zero locations.

RW – Read a 16-bit word from storage to page zero
Subroutines – STTMP, LDTMP.
Length – 26.
Stack – 3.
Input – A = the number of the word to be read. X = the address of the first page zero byte it is to be read into.
Output – Page zero locations X−X+1 hold the value of the word read from store.
Registers changed – None.
Method – The word to be read is at the word storage base address plus double the word number. The word number is therefore doubled, by shifting it left one bit, so that it can be used to index the word storage base address. In word numbers of 128 or more, the left shift will lose into the carry the most significant bit, with a value of 128 that needs to be doubled to 256. In this case, one (representing 256) is added to the high byte of the word storage base address. Because the word storage base address might be altered in this way, interrupts are disabled whilst the word read operation is carried out. The interrupt flag is restored to its original state by the PLP instruction immediately before the return from LDTMP.

RW:	JSR	STTMP	;save regs. in pz.	20	lo	hi
	SEI		;disbl. interrupts as	78		
	ASL	A	;WRDH altered.Double	0A		
	BCC	RWHI	;A for 2-byte indxg.	90	02	
	INC	WRDH	;any carry to WRDH.	E6	1B	
RWHI:	TAY		;index the	A8		
	LDA	(WRDL),Y	;wanted word	B1	1A	
	STA	$00,X	;and move	95	00	
	INY		;two bytes from	C8		
	LDA	(WRDL),Y	;store to page zero	B1	1A	
	STA	$01,X	;indexed by X.	95	01	

	BCC	RWHD	;if WRDH was inc'd	90	02	
	DEC	WRDH	;decrease it back.	C6	1B	
RWHD:	JMP	LDTMP	;return with pz regs.	4C	lo	hi

WW – Write a 16-bit word from page zero to word storage

Subroutines – STTMP, LDTMP.

Length – 26.

Stack – 3.

Input – A = the number of the word to be written. X = the address of the first page zero byte it is to be written from.

Output – The page zero word is placed in the correct word storage locations for its number.

Registers changed – None.

Method – The word is to be written to the word storage base address plus double the word number. This is calculated, with interrupts disabled, as in RW.

WW:	JSR	STTMP	;save regs. in pz.	20	lo	hi
	SEI		;disbl. interrupts as	78		
	ASL	A	;WRDH altered. Double	0A		
	BCC	WWHI	;A for 2-byte indxg.	90	02	
	INC	WRDH	;any carry to WRDH.	E6	1B	
WWHI:	TAY		;index the word	A8		
	LDA	$00,X	;storage destination	B5	00	
	STA	(WRDL),Y	;and move	91	1A	
	INY		;two bytes from pz,	C8		
	LDA	$01,X	;indexed by X, to	B5	01	
	STA	(WRDL),Y	;word storage.	91	1A	
	BCC	WWHD	;if WRDH was inc'd	90	02	
	DEC	WRDH	;decrease it back.	C6	1B	
WWHD:	JMP	LDTMP	;return with pz regs.	4C	lo	hi

Don't worry if the code in these routines for finding addresses seems a little tedious. It is. But nothing imaginative and exciting has been done in computing without a grounding of hard and meticulous work. With these housekeeping chores taken care of, the writing of the other routines that use them will be more interesting.

Chapter Four
Delays

Machine code runs so fast that we soon have to get to grips with slowing it down and controlling it. Nobody would want a 150 mph car that did nothing but 150 mph from start to stop. It is possible to screen and erase, without delay, so quickly that nothing is visible, as some of us blush to remember.

The time taken to complete a microprocessor instruction is measured in cycles and the 6502 instruction cycles (from 2 to 7) are given in the 'Time' column with the instruction set in Appendix A. In some instructions, an extra cycle is added to the standard number if a page boundary is crossed. In these cases, the time taken to execute the instruction depends on its position in memory. In 6500 terminology, a cycle corresponds to a clock pulse, so that a system running at 2 MHz will go through 2 million cycles per second.

The simplest form of delay has only to execute instructions that take the required number of cycles, without having any other effect. Here is an example, assuming no page boundaries are crossed by those instructions that would be affected. The numbers of cycles for instructions and loops are given in place of the usual comments.

DL1S – One second delay at 2 MHz
Subroutines – None.
Length – 42.
Stack – 5.
Input – None.
Output – A delay of 1 second.
Registers changed – None.
Method – The jump to the routine from the main program takes 6
   cycles and the routine itself takes 1999993. Three loop counters,
   called OTR, INR and FYN have values of 251, 0 (to give 256) and
   197 respectively, to control an outer loop, an inner loop and a
   loop for fine adjustments. The number of cycles used by the

routine is determined by the expression 45+OTR*(INR*31+28) +(FYN*5−1).

OTR	EQU	251	;outer loop count.			
INR	EQU	0	;for 256 inner loop count.			
FYN	EQU	197	;fine adjustment loop count.			
DLIS:	PHP		;3		08	
	PHA		;3		48	
	TXA		;2		8A	
	PHA		;3		48	
	TYA		;2		98	
	PHA		;3		48	
	LDY	#OTR	;2		A0	FB
D0:	TYA		;2...................		98	
	PHA		;3	251*	48	
D1:	LDX	#INR	;2		A2	00
D2:	LDY	#5	;2..................	7964	A0	05
D3:	DEY		;2....24 256*		88	
	BNE	D3	;3/2..: 31 : −1		D0	FD
	DEX		;2 =		CA	
	BNE	D2	;3/2............7935		D0	F8
	LDY	#2	;2 −1: =		A0	02
D4:	DEY		;2......9		88	
	BNE	D4	;3/2...:		D0	FD
	PLA		;4 1,:		68	
	TAY		;2 998,		A8	
	DEY		;2 963.		88	
	BNE	D0	;3/2.......................:		D0	EA
	LDY	#FYN	;2		A0	C5
D5:	DEY		;2...984		88	
	BNE	D5	;3/2..:		D0	FD
	PLA		;4		68	
	TAY		;2		A8	
	PLA		;4		68	
	TAX		;2		AA	
	PLA		;4		68	
	PLP		;4		28	
	RTS		;6		60	

For processors running at 1 MHz, OTR set to 126, INR to 255 and FYN to 78 will use 999992 cycles which, with the 6 cycles to jump to the routine, will give a total of 999998. There is no point in worrying about the one or two cycles short of the round million. Counting up cycles like this can give fairly accurate results but not the absolute precision most of us would like. The quartz crystals controlling the clock pulses on most personal computers (that is, all those that we know of) are not absolutely accurate. They have a tolerance, varying with quality, from their rated speed of operation. Because of this, the loop counts are usually decided by experiment. This is what you will have to do for the next delay routine, as it introduces a factor that cannot be measured precisely – the keyboard scanning routine.

The keyboard scanning routine, GETCH, is defined in Chapter 1 and will need to be found in your machine's system software. A word of warning about GETCH's use of the stack. You must find out what this is, as it might be very much greater than you would expect. If you have no adequate documentation of the routine, you can find out its stack use by experiment. Zeroise a number of locations down from the top of page one, then execute your keyboard scanning routine and see how many of the zeroised locations have been overwritten.

Now for the delay. The routine will delay for a given number of hundredths of a second or until a character is input from the keyboard. The number of hundredths of a second delay is given in page zero location DELN and this can be set to 200 ($C8) whilst you determine the value needed, which is put in page zero location DELH, to cause the hundredth of a second delay. If you then set up code to execute INKD 30 times, to aim at a total delay of a minute, and start with DELH at 8, you can adjust this value as necessary to make the total delay as near to a minute as you can get.

INKD – Timed delay while waiting for keyboard input
Subroutines – GETCH to scan the keyboard for input.
Length – 33.
Stack – The greater of GETCH stack requirements or 3.
Input – Delay information in page zero locations DELH and DELN.
Output – Carry = 0: no input, full delay time used.

Carry = 1:input character in page zero location KCH and early exit from the routine.
Registers changed – P.
Method – Registers are stored in TMP store and any change to the carry is also made there at label IDKND. Because of this use of TMP store, GETCH must not corrupt TMPA-P-Y or X. GETCH returns any input character in A or 0 for no input, so the ADC $FF instruction ($FF has a value of −1) will always set the carry if there has been any input or otherwise leave it clear. If there has been input, the ADC #0 instruction after label IDKND will add one back to the character to correct it.

INKD:	CLC		;clear cy = no input.	18		
	JSR	STTMP	;store regs in pz.	20	lo	hi
	CLD		;fix for binary arith.	D8		
	LDX	DELN	;no of 1/100 second.	A6	13	
IDNL:	LDY	DELH	;1/100 s delay factor.	A4	12	
IDHL:	JSR	GETCH	;seek input making cy	20	lo	hi
	ADC	#$FF	;set if not 0 return.	69	FF	
	BCS	IDKND	;end early on input.	B0	08	
	DEY		;else loop till 1/100	88		
	BNE	IDHL	;second is complete.	D0	F6	
	DEX		;loop till wanted no.	CA		
	BNE	IDNL	;of 1/100 secs done.	D0	F1	
	BEQ	IDND	;exit with no input.	F0	06	
IDKND:	INC	TMPP	;set carry in TMPP	E6	05	
	ADC	#0	;to show input. Correct	69	00	
	STA	KCH	;char code to KCH.	85	10	
IDND:	JMP	LDTMP	;return with pz regs.	4C	lo	hi

There is another form of delay. The delay until any key on the keyboard is pressed. There is not much to this, except its usefulness.

WAIT – Wait until a key is pressed
Subroutines – GETCH.
Length – 12.
Stack – 2 + GETCH stack requirements.
Registers changed – None.

WAIT:	PHP		;save the P and	08		
	PHA		;A registers.	48		
W1:	JSR	GETCH	;scan the keyboard.	20	lo	hi
	ORA	#0	;test the A register	09	00	
	BEQ	W1	;and go back if zero.	F0	F9	
	PLA		;recover the A	68		
	PLP		;and P registers.	28		
	RTS		;return.	60		

Chapter Five
Screen Filling and Scrolling

Since the hardware dealing with video display can vary enormously from one computer system to another, it is necessary to review briefly some of the different types which might be encountered.

One type, more common in the 'business' micro than in the 'home' or 'personal' micro, treats the video display exactly as if it were a printer. Character codes have to be sent out through a port and the display system's logic takes over when a character is received. With this type of display one can do little more than output a series of characters and control codes.

By far the most common type of video display to be found on the home computer is that which uses an area of RAM for storing binary codes corresponding to alphanumeric or graphics characters. This area can be accessed directly by the processor in the same way as any other area of Read/Write memory. The only difference lies in the fact that the video logic also reads from this area of memory, the system being designed so that the processor's Read/Write does not conflict with the Read by the display logic. Because of the simple direct relationship between memory locations and points on the screen, this type of display is usually known as a *memory-mapped display*.

In monochromatic, low resolution display systems, just one byte of memory is enough to hold all the information required by one screen character location. The text display routines in this book are designed primarily for such a system, though the display area definition does allow for some flexibility.

In more sophisticated systems attributes such as colour, degree of brightness, underlining, flashing and inverse characters have to be considered. A system might support high resolution graphics where each dot on the screen can be lit or unlit. All of these highly desirable features require extra memory to be allocated to the display and obviously make for more complexity in putting text or graphics on the screen. Where, in our routines FILL, PCHAR and SCROL, we simply store a byte in video RAM to cause a character to appear in its corresponding screen location, in more complex systems you might need to do some other processing. You would probably do this by calling a routine, that is already in your systems software, to display a character.

Filling the screen

In the most simple memory-mapped display, screen memory is organised in such a way that each next higher byte has a screen location which is one character to the right of the preceding one. This means that a string of character codes stored sequentially in screen memory will appear on the screen running from left to right.

The routine we will consider below can be used to clear the screen but, because it takes account of the information in the current display area, will fill with the character in page zero location PCH, the screen area defined either to the right or left, up or down from the home address, with the possibility of skipping columns and or rows.

FILL – Fill the display area with the character in page zero PCH
Subroutines – PSHZM, PARAM, STTMP, TFRZZ, ADCZZ, LDTMP.
Length – 57.
Stack – 7. *User Stack* – 9.
Input – A definition of the screen area to be filled is in the current display area. The character used for filling is in page zero location PCH.
Output – The screen filled with the character as specified.
Registers changed – None.
Method – The address where the character is to be placed, starting at the home address, is held in user register A. An outer loop, from label FLLL to the BNE FLLL instruction, updates user register A to point in turn to the screen lines to be filled. An inner loop, from label FLCL to the BNE FLCL instruction, updates user register A to point in turn to the columns of the line to be filled and stores the filling character.

```
FILL:   JSR     PSHZM       ;save user A & regs.     20   lo    hi
        EQB     TMPA,$3F    ;on the user stack.      04   3F
        CLD                 ;for binary arith.       D8
```

	LDY	#0	;zero indx throughout.	A0	00	
	LDA	PCH	;get filling char.	A5	11	
	JSR	TFRZZ	;move home addr to	20	lo	hi
	EQB	DHL,UAL	;user reg A pointer.	28	08	
	LDX	DLN	;X is line high index	A6	2B	
	INX		;+1 = line count.	E8		
FLLL:	JSR	PSHZM	;save line start addr.	20	lo	hi
	EQB	TMPA,$38	;and line count.	04	38	
	LDX	DCN	;X is char high index	A6	2A	
	INX		;+1 = character count.	E8		
FLCL:	STA	(UAL),Y	;char to screen addr.	91	08	
	CLC		;point to next screen	18		
	JSR	ADCZZ	;address by adding	20	lo	hi
	EQB	UAL,DCDL	;char byte difference.	08	2C	
	DEX		;repeat for all chars	CA		
	BNE	FLCL	;in a screen line.	D0	F5	
	JSR	PULZM	;restore line count	20	lo	hi
	EQB	TMPA,$38	;and line start addr.	04	38	
	CLC		;point to next line	18		
	JSR	ADCZZ	;by adding DLDL-H	20	lo	hi
	EQB	UAL,DLDL	;(line byte diff.).	08	2E	
	DEX		;repeat for all lines	CA		
	BNE	FLLL	;in the screen area.	D0	DF	
	JSR	PULZM	;restore registers	20	lo	hi
	EQB	TMPA,$3F	;and user A then	04	3F	
	RTS		;return.	60		

If you are going to use FILL to clear the screen, you will be using it a lot and it will be worth having a separate little routine to set everything up for this special use of FILL. The routine given next can be entered either at the label CLRDA, when the display area whose number is given in the A register will be cleared, or at the label CLCDA, when the screen as defined in the current display area is cleared.

CLRDA or CLCDA – Clear a defined display area

Subroutines – FILL, PSHZM, PARAM, STTMP, TFRZZ, ADCZZ, LDTMP and in addition, when entered at CLRDA, RDAP and HOME.

Length – 14.

Stack – 7. *User Stack* – 9.

Input – The A register holds the display area number for CLRDA; the current display area must already define the screen to be cleared for entry at CLCDA.

Output – The screen area, either as numbered in A or defined in the current display area, is cleared.

Registers changed – None.

Method – The CLRDA entry uses the value in the A register to get new display area parameters into the current display area, by a call to RDAP. In either case, $20 (ASCII space) is moved to page zero location PCH, from where FILL puts it into every location defined in the current display area.

CLRDA:	JSR	RDAP	;get area;home cursor.	20	lo	hi
CLCDA:	PHP		;save A and P whilst	08		
	PHA		;putting ASCII	48		
	LDA	#32	;space code into	A9	20	
	STA	PCH	;character to print.	85	11	
	PLA		;recover A & P regs.	68		
	PLP		;and exit via FILL	28		
	JMP	FILL	;to space fill area.	4C	lo	hi

With CLRDA and all its associated subroutines, plus WAIT and GETCH from Chapter 4, we can run a small experimental program, EXP1, using FILL to show some differently defined display areas in use. In addition to the subroutines, you must provide for a user stack of at least 9 bytes anywhere in memory, with its highest address in USPL-H. You will need memory for 7 sets of display area parameters, each of 8 bytes, with their base address in DAPL-H. Other page zero locations for temporary storage, user registers, the character to print, display information and the current display area, as described in Chapter 3, will be used by the routines.

Assuming a screen of 40 columns by 25 rows, with a normal character byte difference of 1 and a single line byte difference of 40, with its top left character address at $6000, 7 sets of display area parameters (if starting at address $2300) would be set up as follows, with all values not in brackets given in hexadecimal:

Address	Contents								
2300	00	60	27	18	01	00	28	00	
2308	DC	60	12	12	01	00	28	00	
2310	4D	62	09	09	01	00	D8	FF	($FFD8 = −40)
2318	4D	62	09	09	FF	FF	D8	FF	($FFFF = −1)
2320	4D	62	09	09	01	00	28	00	
2328	4D	62	09	09	FF	FF	28	00	
2330	DC	60	06	06	03	00	78	00	

The first set of parameters, for display area 0, defines the whole screen, with the home address at its top left-hand corner. Parameters for display area 1 define a 19 column by 19 row window, with a top left corner at column 20 row 5, a bottom right corner at column 38 row 23 and a home address at the top left corner. Display areas 2 to 5 all have their home address at the centre of the window, with area 2 displaying to the right and upwards, 3 to the left and upwards, 4 to the right and downwards and 5 to the left and downwards. Display area 6 defines every third column and row of the window from the home address at its top left corner.

EXP1:	LDY	#7	;count of disp. areas.	A0	07	
	LDX	#$30	;starting fill char 0.	A2	30	
	LDA	#0	;starting disp. area.	A9	00	
	CLC		;clear carry.	18		
	CLD		;clear for biny arith.	D8		
EXP1A:	STX	PCH	;put fill char in pz.	86	61	
	JSR	RDAP	;get next disp. area	20	lo	hi
	JSR	FILL	;and fill it.	20	lo	hi
	JSR	WAIT	;wait for any key.	20	lo	hi
	ADC	#1	;get next disp. no.	69	01	
	DEX		;change fill char.	CA		
	DEY		;decrement count.	88		
	BNE	EXP1A	;repeat for all disps.	D0	EF	
	TYA		;A = disp. area 0.	98		
	JSR	CLRDA	;clear screen.	20	lo	hi
	JSR	WAIT	;wait for any key.	20	lo	hi
	JMP	($FFFC)	;jump to restart sys.	6C	FC	FF

The program fills each of the 7 display areas in turn, waiting after each fill for any key on the keyboard to be pressed. The whole screen is filled with zeros, the window with solidi (ASCII $2F), the top right quarter of the window with dots, the top left quarter with minus signs, the bottom right quarter with commas, the bottom left quarter with plus signs and then every third column and row of the window with asterisks. The program then clears the screen and waits for a key to be pressed before jumping to your system's restart procedure.

Scrolling

Software scrolling is done by moving all characters in the display video RAM, column by column towards the home address. Figure 5.1 shows the movement of the first 50 characters in scrolling

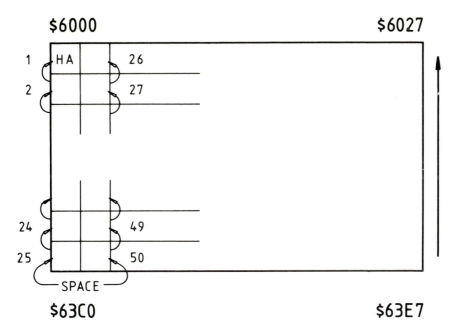

Fig. 5.1. Scrolling up.

upwards in display area 0, defined earlier in the chapter. Now look at 3 more sets of display area parameters, 7 to 9, for the whole screen:

Address	Contents							
2338	00	60	18	27	28	00	01	00
2340	E7	63	27	18	FF	FF	D8	FF
2348	E7	63	18	27	D8	FF	FF	FF

Display area 7, with the home address still at the top left character position but with the character high index 24, the line high index 39, the character byte difference 40 and the line byte difference 1, will scroll left as shown in Fig. 5.2. In display areas 8 and 9 the home address is at the bottom right corner and the character and line high indices and byte differences are set for scrolling down and right respectively. It is the definition of the display area that determines how scrolling is done. With suitable adjustments of the character and line high indices and byte differences, upwards, downwards, right and left scrolling could be done from home addresses at the top right and bottom left screen positions by this same routine SCROL.

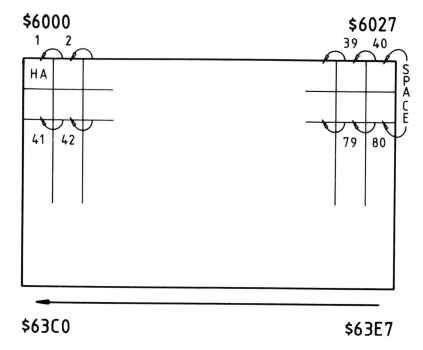

$6000   **$6027**

$63C0   **$63E7**

Fig. 5.2. Scrolling left.

SCROL – Scroll the current display area
Subroutines – PSHZM, PULZM, PARAM, STTMP, LDTMP.
Length – 93.
Stack – 7. *User Stack –* 8.
Input – Parameters for the display area to be scrolled must be set in
the current display area.
Output – The display area is scrolled by one row towards home,
clearing the last row.
Registers changed – None.
Method – In the first column, the character from line 1 is put in line
0, the character from line 2 is put in line 1 and so on until the
character from the last line is put in the last line but one and a
space is put in the last line. This process is repeated for all other
columns in turn.

SCROL:	JSR	PSHZM	;save user A & B and	20	lo hi
	EQB	TMPA,$FF	;regs on user stack.	04	FF
	CLD		;for binary arith.	D8	
	LDY	#0	;zero indx throughout.	A0	00
	LDA	DHL	;move home address	A5	28
	STA	UAL	;from current display	85	08

	LDA	DHH	;area to source	A5	29	
	STA	UAH	;pointer (user A).	85	09	
	LDX	DCN	;X = character count.	A6	2A	
	INX		;= no. of chrs in row.	E8		
SCRCL:	TXA		;save	8A		
	PHA		;character	48		
	LDA	UAL	;(column)	A5	08	
	PHA		;start address	48		
	LDA	UAH	;and character	A5	09	
	PHA		;count.	48		
	LDX	DLN	;X = count of lines −1.	A6	2B	
	BEQ	SCRZ	;skip if single line.	F0	1C	
SCRLL:	LDA	UAL	;move source	A5	08	
	STA	UBL	;pointer into	85	0A	
	LDA	UAH	;destination	A5	09	
	STA	UBH	;pointer.	85	0B	
	CLC		;source	18		
	LDA	UAL	;pointer	A5	08	
	ADC	DLDL	;moved to	65	2E	
	STA	UAL	;next line	85	08	
	LDA	UAH	;by adding	A5	09	
	ADC	DLDH	;DLDL-H	65	2F	
	STA	UAH	;(line byte diff).	85	09	
	LDA	(UAL),Y	;move char one line	B1	08	
	STA	(UBL),Y	;nearer home line.	91	0A	
	DEX		;do for whole column	CA		
	BNE	SCRLL	;of characters.	D0	E4	
SCRZ:	LDA	#32	;space into character	A9	20	
	STA	(UAL),Y	;in the last line.	91	08	
	PLA		;restore	68		
	STA	UAH	;line 0	85	09	
	PLA		;address	68		
	STA	UAL	;and	85	08	
	PLA		;character	68		
	TAX		;count.	AA		
	CLC		;set source	18		
	LDA	UAL	;pointer	A5	08	
	ADC	DCDL	;to next	65	2C	
	STA	UAL	;character on	85	08	
	LDA	UAH	;line 0 by	A5	09	
	ADC	DCDH	;adding DCDL-H	65	2D	
	STA	UAH	;(char byte diff).	85	09	
	DEX		;do for no. of chars	CA		
	BNE	SCRCL	;in the display area.	D0	BC	
	JSR	PULZM	;restore regs and	20	lo	hi

```
        EQB    TMPA,$FF   ;user A and B.        04    FF
        RTS               ;return.              60
```

Using our utility routines **TFRZZ, PSHZM, TFRZZ, ADCZZ, PULZM** and **ADCZZ** with appropriate parameters in place of lines 5–8, 11–16, 19–22, 24–29, 36–41 and 43–48, SCROL can be written in 67 bytes. But calling subroutines, particularly robust ones which preserve all registers, incurs a time penalty. Subroutines which occur in often repeated loops and nested loops (loops within loops) can visibly slow down the action to what might be an unacceptable level. There is a marked difference in the speed of scrolling avoiding and using the utility routines. Try it and see. Looping itself incurs a time penalty and, to avoid this in producing some special effects, the same code is sometimes repeated many times instead.

You can see how much processing is involved in software scrolling. Some systems have what is known as 'hardware scrolling'. Here the start address of the memory scanned to produce the display is taken from a register, which can be altered by program to produce extremely fast scrolling. This is a feature to look for if you are interested in producing stunning visual effects.

Chapter Six
Displaying Text

It seems a simple enough matter to display a character on a memory-mapped screen. Just store it in the right screen address. This chapter is about keeping track of the right screen address without having to bring to mind the actual address of each character displayed.

The display area being worked in, which can be the whole or any rectangular part of the screen, has been defined by display area parameters brought into the current display area. When parameters are brought into the current display area, display area information is set to zero for the next screen action to operate at the home address.

To cause the next screen action to operate away from the home address, we have routines for the basic movements of the cursor, forwards and backwards one character and forwards and backwards one line. We keep track of the cursor by a character index and a line index and by accumulating the character byte displacement from the start of the line and the line byte displacement from the start of the screen.

There is no input and output specific to these routines, which alter the display information in page zero and leave all the processor's registers unchanged.

CFC – Cursor forward by one character unless at the last character of the line
Subroutines – ADCZZ, PARAM, STTMP, LDTMP.
Length – 19.
Stack – 9.

CFC:	PHP		;save the processor	08	
	PHA		;status and accum.	48	
	LDA	CCN	;check if cursor at	A5	22
	CMP	DCN	;last char on line,	C5	2A
	PLA		;restore A and exit	68	
	BCS	CFCND	;immediately if it is.	B0	08

	INC	CCN	;else move char index	E6	22	
	CLD		;to next char and add	D8		
	JSR	ADCZZ	;character byte diff.	20	lo	hi
	EQB	CCDL,DCDL	;to char byte dispmt.	24	2C	
CFCND:	PLP		;restore processor	28		
	RTS		;status and return.	60		

CBC – Cursor back by one character unless at character 0
Subroutines – SBCZZ, PARAM, STTMP, LDTMP.
Length – 18.
Stack – 9.

CBC:	PHP		;save the processor	08		
	PHA		;status and accum.	48		
	LDA	CCN	;exit immediately if	A5	22	
	BEQ	CBCND	;cursor at line start	F0	09	
	DEC	CCN	;else back-up char	C6	22	
	CLD		;index and take char	D8		
	SEC		;byte difference from	38		
	JSR	SBCZZ	;character byte	20	lo	hi
	EQB	CCDL,DCDL	;displacement.	24	2C	
CBCND:	PLA		;restore accumulator	68		
	PLP		;and processor status	28		
	RTS		;and return.	60		

CFL – Cursor forward by one line, scrolling if at the last line
Subroutines – SCROL, PSHZM, PULZM, PARAM, STTMP,
*   LDTMP, ADCZZ.*
Length – 23.
Stack – 11. User Stack – 8.

CFL:	PHP		;save the processor	08		
	PHA		;status and accum.	48		
	LDA	CLN	;test for	A5	23	
	CMP	DLN	;last line.	C5	2B	
	PLA		;restore accumulator.	68		
	BCC	CFLD	;if on last line then	90	04	
	PLP		;leave on last line	28		
	JMP	SCROL	;but exit via SCROL.	4C	lo	hi
CFLD:	INC	CLN	;else move line index	E6	23	
	CLD		;to next line and add	D8		
	JSR	ADCZZ	;line byte difference	20	lo	hi
	EQB	CLDL,DLDL	;to line byte displ.	26	2E	
	PLP		;restore processor	28		
	RTS		;status and return.	60		

CBL – Cursor back by one line unless on line 0
Subroutines – SBCZZ, PARAM, STTMP, LDTMP.
Length – 18.
Stack – 9.

CBL:	PHP		;save the processor	08		
	PHA		;status and accum.	48		
	LDA	CLN	;exit immediately if	A5	23	
	BEQ	CBLND	;cursor on line 0	F0	09	
	DEC	CLN	;else back-up line	C6	23	
	CLD		;index and take line	D8		
	SEC		;byte difference from	38		
	JSR	SBCZZ	;line byte	20	lo	hi
	EQB	CLDL,DLDL	;displacement.	26	2E	
CBLND:	PLA		;restore processor	68		
	PLP		;status and accum.	28		
	RTS		;and return	60		

Another routine, CR, is useful in reflecting printer output to the screen, and sets the cursor to the start of the current line, imitating a carriage return.

CR – Set the cursor to the start of the current line
Subroutines – None.
Length – 13.
Stack – 2.

CR:	PHP		;save the processor	08	
	PHA		;status and accum.	48	
	LDA	#0	;use A to clear the	A9	00
	STA	CCN	;character index	85	22
	STA	CCDL	;and character	85	24
	STA	CCDH	;byte displacement.	85	25
	PLA		;restore accumulator	68	
	PLP		;and processor status	28	
	RTS		;and return.	60	

With CR and CFL we can set the cursor to the start of the next line, imitating the carriage return and line feed.

CRLF – Set the cursor to the start of the next line, scrolling if at the last line
Subroutines – CR, CFL, SCROL, PSHZM, PULZM, PARAM,
  STTMP, LDTMP, ADCZZ.
Length – 6.
Stack – 11. *User Stack* – 8.

CRLF:	JSR	CR	;carriage return.	20	lo	hi
	JMP	CFL	;line feed.	4C	lo	hi

Since the cursor is tracked by character and line byte displacements, a routine is needed to calculate the actual cursor address, which is the home address plus the line byte displacement plus the character byte displacement.

CADDR – Get the current cursor address into user register A
Subroutines – TFRZZ, ADCZZ, PARAM, STTMP, LDTMP.
Length – 21.
Stack – 8.

CADDR:	PHP		;save procr status.	08		
	CLD		;for binary arith.	D8		
	JSR	TFRZZ	;move home address to	20	lo	hi
	EQB	DHL,UAL	;user register A.	28	08	
	CLC		;clear carry and add	18		
	JSR	ADCZZ	;line byte displ.	20	lo	hi
	EQB	UAL,CLDL	;giving current line.	08	26	
	CLC		;clear carry and add	18		
	JSR	ADCZZ	;char. byte displ.	20	lo	hi
	EQB	UAL,CCDL	;giving char. place	08	24	
	PLP		;on line. Restore	28		
	RTS		;status and return.	60		

Since we have organised things to display the character which is in page zero location PCH, a routine to store that character at the current cursor position comes next.

PCHAR – Display PCH at the current cursor position, updating the cursor as far as the line end
Subroutines – PSHZM, CADDR, PULZM, PARAM, STTMP, LDTMP, TFRZZ, ADCZZ.
Length – 22.
Stack – 10. *User Stack* – 5.

PCHAR:	JSR	PSHZM	;save user A and P,A	20	lo	hi
	EQB	TMPA,$37	;and Y on user stack.	04	37	
	JSR	CADDR	;user A = cursor addr.	20	lo	hi
	LDY	#0	;zero index it and	A0	00	
	LDA	PCH	;store display char	A5	11	
	STA	(UAL),Y	;in cursor location.	91	08	
	JSR	PULZM	;restore Y,A and P	20	lo	hi
	EQB	TMPA,$37	;and user register A.	04	37	
	JMP	CFC	;move cursor 1 char.	4C	lo	hi

PCHAR limits cursor movement to the current line, as might sometimes be required. This next routine uses PCHAR but allows for cursor movement to the next line and also for scrolling after displaying at the last character position of the screen.

AUTOP – Display PCH at the current cursor position, with automatic CRLF and SCROL

Subroutines – PCHAR, CRLF, PSHZM, CADDR, PULZM, PARAM, STTMP, LDTMP, TFRZZ, ADCZZ, CR, CFL and SCROL.

Length – 17.

Stack – 14. *User Stack –* 8.

AUTOP:	PHP		;save the processor	08		
	PHA		;status and accum.	48		
	LDA	CCN	;set carry if cursor	A5	22	
	CMP	DCN	;at last char on line.	C5	2A	
	PLA		;restore accumulator.	68		
	JSR	PCHAR	;display character.	20	lo	hi
	BCC	AUTND	;if carry set, do	90	03	
	JSR	CRLF	;CRLF scrolling if	20	lo	hi
AUTND:	PLP		;needed. Restore P	28		
	RTS		;and return.	60		

From the routines HOME in Chapter 3 (to home the cursor), CLRDA in Chapter 5 (to clear the current display area), and the routines in this chapter (to move the cursor and display a character), a routine is assembled to select an operation to either display an ASCII character or move the cursor.

PSLCT – Select an operation to display a character or move the cursor

Subroutines – ADCZI, AUTOP, HOME, CFC, CBC, CFL, CBL, CR, CRFL, CLCDA, PCHAR, PSHZM, CADDR, PULZM, PARAM, STTMP, LDTMP, TFRZZ, ADCZZ, SBCZZ, FILL and SCROL.

Length – 72.

Stack – 14. *User Stack –* 9.

Input – The routine operates on the value of the byte at page zero location PCH. If this is an ASCII character in the range $20 to $7E it is displayed at the current cursor position and the cursor is moved on one character, with scrolling if needed. Values of $01 to $08 cause action as follows:

$01 home the cursor		$02 cursor forward one character	
$03 cursor back one character		$04 cursor forward one line	
$05 cursor back one line		$06 carriage return	
$07 carriage return/line feed		$08 clear the current display area	

Output – According to the input value. Values not specified in the input section are ignored.

Registers changed – None.

Method – Values in PCH of $00, $09 to $1F or greater than $7E are invalid. The CMP (compare) instruction, which sets the carry when the value in memory is less than or equal to the accumulator, is used to filter them out. For a valid ASCII value, A is set to zero; otherwise it keeps the valid value of PCH. The address of the last byte of the ADCZI instruction is in TMPL-H when 22 is added to it so that it points to the base address of the jump table at JPTBL. The value of A times 3 is then added to this base address so that TMPL-H points to the instruction to jump to the specific routine selected. This method, of selecting one of many instructions from a table, saves having to provide for testing for each value of A individually and means that all the jump instructions are selected equally quickly.

PSLCT:	PHP		;save the processor	08	
	PHA		;status and accum.	48	
	CLD		;for binary arith.	D8	
	LDA	PCH	;get char and test	A5	11
	BEQ	PSLNV	;for invalid if A=0	F0	23
	CMP	#127	;or greater	C9	7F
	BCS	PSLNV	;than 126 ($7E).	B0	1F
	CMP	#32	;skip if A < 32	C9	20
	BCC	PSLCC	;else, when 32–126,	90	02
	LDA	#0	;set A = 0.	A9	00
PSLCC:	CMP	#9	;invalid if A now >8.	C9	09
	BCS	PSLNV	;add offset to return	B0	15
	JSR	ADCZI	;addr in TMPL-H so	20	lo hi
	EQB	TMPL,$16	;is base addr of jump	02	16
	ASL	A	;table.ADCZI left A	0A	
	ADC	TMPA	;in TMPA so now A*3	65	04
	ADC	TMPL	;(3-byte entries)	65	02
	STA	TMPL	;added to base addr	85	02
	BCC	PSLV	;giving correct jump	90	02
	INC	TMPH	;place in jump table.	E6	03
PSLV:	PLA		;restore A & P and	68	
	PLP		;jump to correct	28	
	JMP	(TMPL)	;action via table.	6C	02 00

PSLNV:	PLA		;restore A and P	68		
	PLP		;registers and	28		
	RTS		;return no action.	60		
JPTBL:	JMP	AUTOP	;display character.	4C	lo	hi
	JMP	HOME	;home cursor.	4C	lo	hi
	JMP	CFC	;cursor f'ward 1 char.	4C	lo	hi
	JMP	CBC	;cursor back 1 char.	4C	lo	hi
	JMP	CFL	;cursor f'ward 1 line.	4C	lo	hi
	JMP	CBL	;cursor back 1 line.	4C	lo	hi
	JMP	CR	;carriage return.	4C	lo	hi
	JMP	CRLF	;car. ret./line feed.	4C	lo	hi
	JMP	CLCDA	;clear display area.	4C	lo	hi

Having taken care of displaying a character, we can move on to displaying a string of characters, which can include codes for cursor movements as well as text. The display will take place within the current display area and the character string to be displayed will have been set up in RAM as described in Chapter 3, which also gives the routines for getting string information into the user registers:

PSBS – Display a string (or substring) of characters

Subroutines – PSLCT, ADCZI, AUTOP, HOME, CFC, CBC, CFL, CBL, CR, CRFL, CLCDA, PCHAR, PSHZM, CADDR, PULZM, PARAM, STTMP, LDTMP, TFRZZ, ADCZZ, SBCZZ, FILL and SCROL.

Length – 31.

Stack – 16. *User Stack* – 17.

Input – A = the string number. X holds the number of the character from which the display is to start, except, when X = 0, display starts from character 1. Y holds the number of the character the display is to go to, with the exception that, when Y = 0 or would go beyond the end of the string, display is to the last character of the string.

Output – The specified character string displayed.

Registers changed – None.

Method – The character at the address in user register A, as indexed by Y, is displayed via PCH. The value input in X or 1 is put into page zero location UBH and the value input in Y, or that which will index the last character of the string, in UBL. When indexing the string, Y starts with the value in UBH and finishes with the value in UBL. Since display is via AUTOP in PSLCT it is kept within the current display area with scrolling as necessary.

PSBS:	JSR	PSHZM	;save regs and user A	20	lo	hi
	EQB	TMPA,$FF	;& B on user stack.	04	FF	
	JSR	SBSTR	;get substring info.	20	lo	hi
	LDY	UBH	;get 'from' and dec	A4	0B	
	DEY		;for test with 'to'.	88		
PSBSL:	CPY	UBL	;end if 'from'	C4	0A	
	BCS	PSBND	;> or = 'to',	B0	0A	
	INY		;else index next char	C8		
	LDA	(UAL),Y	;and move to PCH for	B1	08	
	STA	PCH	;display or control	85	11	
	JSR	PSLCT	;character. Repeat	20	lo	hi
	BCC	PSBSL	;for all substring.	90	F2	
PSBND:	JSR	PULZM	;restore user B	20	lo	hi
	EQB	TMPA,$FF	;& A and registers	04	FF	
	RTS		;and return.	60		

Now is the time to experiment on your own with these display routines. The demonstration program, EXP1, in Chapter 5 showed the power of the routine FILL used in conjunction with the display area parameters. Those same parameters are used by the character and string display routines in this chapter. In addition, SBSTR from Chapter 3 and PSBS, which calls SBSTR, require the setting up of a character string (which can include cursor movement codes) and the base address of the RAM reserved for character strings to be in page zero locations STRL-H.

Exchanging character and line indices and byte differences will result in strings being displayed vertically. Doubling the line byte difference (and halving the line index to compensate) will result in double line spacing. You can get double character spacing by a similar attack on the character byte difference.

With a little ingenuity you can use these routines to display messages diagonally across the screen or in any direction you wish.

Chapter Seven
Matching Input

This is about a routine to compare a string of one or more characters with elements of an array. The formats of both strings and arrays were given in Chapter 3. We are going to see how the MATCH routine is used to check information given via the keyboard; something we often want to do. Remember that page zero locations STRL-H and ARRL-H hold the base addresses of strings and arrays respectively. Keyboard input will have been placed in a string of appropriate length and an array will have been set up whose elements comprise all acceptable responses to the prompt for that input.

MATCH – Compare a string with elements of an array, returning the position of the string in the array if a match is found

Subroutines – PSHZM, STRNG, TFRZZ, ARRAY, PULZM, PARAM, STTMP, LDTMP, LDZE, MUG, ADCZZ.

Length – 69.

Stack – 18. *User Stack* – 8.

Input – X holds the number of the string to be matched. Y holds the number of the array of responses.

Output – When a match found, A = the position of the string in the array. A = 0 when no match.

Registers changed – A.

Method – At label MTCTL, user register A points to the length byte of the string; user register C points to the byte preceding an element of the array; UBL holds the string length for putting into index Y; UBH holds the number of elements in the array and X holds the number (from 1 upwards) of the array element being tested. Working from the last character to the first, the array element byte is compared to the corresponding byte of the string. If there is a mismatch, the string length is added to user register C so that it points to the byte preceding the next element in the array, which is then compared. If all bytes of an array element match the string, a jump is made to label MTCND with the matching element number in X. If all array elements have been tested without matching the string, X is set to zero before the label MTCND.

MATCH:	PHP		;save status register.	08		
	CLD		;for binary arith.	D8		
	JSR	PSHZM	;save user C,B & A	20	lo	hi
	EQB	TMPY,$FF	;& X & Y on user stk.	06	FF	
	TXA		;get addr & length of	8A		
	JSR	STRNG	;string X. Move	20	lo	hi
	JSR	TFRZZ	;string address	20	lo	hi
	EQB	UAL,UCL	;to user C.	08	0C	
	LDX	#0	;X is element count.	A2	00	
	TYA		;array no to A,string	98		
	LDY	UBL	;length to Y & exit	A4	0A	
	BEQ	MTCND	;if no strg to match.	F0	26	
	JSR	ARRAY	;else get array info	20	lo	hi
	CPY	UBL	;& exit if string X	C4	0A	
	BNE	MTCND	;wrong length to list.	D0	1F	
MTCTL:	INX		;next listed string.	E8		
	LDY	UBL	;index strings from	A4	0A	
MTCSL:	LDA	(UCL),Y	;end & compare bytes,	B1	0C	
	CMP	(UAL),Y	;end loop if unequal	D1	08	
	BNE	MTCNM	;else loop till bytes	D0	05	
	DEY		;don't match or all	88		
	BNE	MTCSL	;match with X=positn	D0	F7	
	BEQ	MTCND	;in str list of match.	F0	11	
MTCNM:	CLC		;add string length to	18		
	LDA	UAL	;user B register	A5	08	
	ADC	UBL	;to move the	65	0A	
	STA	UAL	;pointer to the	85	08	
	BCC	MTCXT	;next string in	90	02	
	INC	UAH	;the string list.	E6	09	
MTCXT:	CPX	UBH	;repeat till all str	E4	0B	
	BNE	MTCTL	;checked. Position	D0	E3	
	LDX	#0	;is 0 for no match.	A2	00	
MTCND:	TXA		;put position in A.	8A		
	JSR	PULZM	;restore Y & X and	20	lo	hi
	EQB	TMPY,$FF	;user A, B & C.	06	FF	
	PLP		;restore processor	28		
	RTS		;status and return.	60		

Suppose your program is offering a choice of application from Power Station Control, Inter Galaxy Rover, Slaughterer, Treasure Trip and Escape From Monday, by keying in the initial character P, I, S, T or E. Your array, in hexadecimal will be:

01 05 50 49 53 54 45

to represent one-character elements (five of them) as listed. A call to MATCH will check the character put into a string from the keyboard against the elements of the array and, if a permissible choice has been made, return with the position in the array of the character selected.

Where a month has been selected by keying in its first three characters to a string and then checking this against the array:

03 0C 4A 41 4E 46 45 42 4D 41 52 41 50 52 4D 41 59 4A 55 4E
     4A 55 4C 41 55 47 53 45 50 4F 43 54 4E 4F 56 44 45 43

the position in the array returned, of 1 to 12, gives a useful binary month. If it later turned out that month 1 was to be April instead of January, no code would have to be changed – just the order of the strings in the array.

The string position could be used to index a table of code addresses, as was done in the PSLCT routine in the last chapter, to cause processing to be carried out according to the selected option. Since the string position could be a conversion of other codes, the cursor movement and other control codes in PSLCT could have been any other values outside the ASCII character range, converted from an array used by MATCH to the jump table indexing values 1 to 8.

Chapter Eight
Prompting

Prompting in this context means asking for information to be given from the keyboard, until usable information is received. This involves checking that the information given is, in fact, usable and warning if it is not.

The PROMPT routine

At the heart of this application is the routine, PRMPT. Quite short in itself, PRMPT depends on many of the other routines covered so far, as shown in the documentation. Because of this, we will just run through the general system requirements that have to be met, in addition to those specific to PRMPT, for the routine to be run successfully:

(1) Addresses of the user stack, RAM reserved for strings and RAM reserved for display area parameters must have been set in page zero locations USPL-H, STRL-H and DAPL-H.
(2) The factor which gives a delay of 1 hundredth of a second on your system should have been set in page zero location DELH, as described in Chapter 4.
(3) The number of hundredths of a second delay you want between the display of each character of the prompt message must be set in DELN. $0A (decimal 10) is about right for this.

The prompt is a revolving message on one line, usually the bottom, of the screen. This looks interesting and allows messages of any size to be displayed in the same small area. The message is displayed until a character is given from the keyboard. Then the start address of the message, its last character index and current character index are left in the prompt information page zero locations. By this means, the message display can be resumed where it left off, if another character is expected in reply to the prompt.

PRMPT uses the current display area, to which appropriate parameters have to be moved before the routine is entered. To get a single row scrolling left, display area parameters have to be set correctly for your particular system. To the ten sets of display area parameters defined in Chapter 5, for a 40 column by 25 row screen, the addition of this next set of parameters would scroll a circular message on the bottom line.

Address	Contents
2350	C0 63 00 27 28 00 01 00

This defines a home address at the bottom left screen character position, a character (in place of line) high index of 0, a line (in place of character) high index of 39 ($27), a character byte difference of 40 ($0028) and a line byte difference of 1 ($0001).

With a suitable prompt message string set in RAM, the routine can be entered:

PRMPT – Print a circular message until a character is given from the keyboard

Subroutines – PSHZM, STRNG, TFRZZ, INKD, PSLCT, PULZM, PARAM, STTMP, LDTMP, GETCH, ADCZI, AUTOP, HOME, CFC, CBC, CFL, CBL, CR, CRFL, CLCDA, PCHAR, CADDR, ADCZZ, SBCZZ, FILL, SCROL.

Length – 51.

Stack – 16 + any stack in excess of 14 bytes required by GETCH.

User Stack – 17.

Input – A = prompt message string number. The carry is set for the prompt to start from the beginning of the message or reset for the message to be continued from where it previously left off.

Output – The character keyed in is in page zero location KCH. The prompt message string address, last character index and current character index are in page zero locations PRAL-H, PRT and PRF.

Registers changed – None.

Method – If the carry was set on entry, string information is set in prompt information locations PRAL-H, PRT and PRF via user A and B registers, from labels PRNEW to PRKRQ. This is also done at every end of the prompt message. From label PRKRQ to

PRND, input is sought from the keyboard, for the number of hundredths of a second given in page zero location DELN. If a character has been given, there is a return from the routine with the output specified. Otherwise a character from the prompt message (at the address in PRAL-H indexed by Y) is put into page zero location PCH and displayed on the screen by PSLCT, with scrolling to the left at the end of the line. This display of prompt message characters continues until a character is given from the keyboard.

PRMPT:	JSR	PSHZM	;save regs and user	20	lo	hi
	EQB	TMPA,$FF	;A & B on user stack.	04	FF	
	TAX		;save string no in X.	AA		
	BCC	PRKRQ	;get new string info.	90	0E	
PRNEW:	TXA		;if cy set on entry	8A		
	JSR	STRNG	;or string end found.	20	lo	hi
	JSR	TFRZZ	;move string	20	lo	hi
	EQB	UAL,PRAL	;information from the	08	14	
	JSR	TFRZZ	;user registers to	20	lo	hi
	EQB	UBL,PRT	;prompt information.	0A	16	
PRKRQ:	JSR	INKD	;seek input and exit	20	lo	hi
	BCS	PRND	;if a char is input.	B0	12	
	LDY	PRF	;else get string char	A4	17	
	LDA	(PRAL),Y	;index and move char	B1	14	
	STA	PCH	;to PCH for print	85	11	
	JSR	PSLCT	;or control.	20	lo	hi
	CPY	PRT	;test for last char	C4	16	
	INY		;before indexing next	C8		
	STY	PRF	;and storing index.	84	17	
	BCC	PRKRQ	;loop if not string	90	EB	
	BCS	PRNEW	;end else get new inf	B0	DB	
PRND:	JSR	PULZM	;restore user B & A	20	lo	hi
	EQB	TMPA,$FF	;and processor regs	04	FF	
	RTS		;and return.	60		

Here is a bit of code to look at PRMPT with. It assumes that the parameters for a bottom line, left scrolling message are in display area table 10, the whole screen parameters in table 0 and the screen window parameters (as defined in Chapter 5) still in table 1. In addition to the requirements of PRMPT, the routines CLRDA, RDAP and DLIS will be needed as well as an extra 16 bytes of the processor's stack.

Character string 0, to be used later, will be a dummy 12-character string to take keyboard input for matching with an array. Character string 1 will hold the prompt message. In this example, the actual characters of the message string are shown, with % used to denote a space, rather than their ASCII codes. The string numbers (in the left-hand column) and string lengths are given in hexadecimal:

```
00    0C(string of 12 characters reserved for input)
01    2FKEY%IN%THE%FIRST%THREE%LETTERS%OF%THE%MONTH%%%%
```

The base address of RAM you have reserved for strings must be set in page zero locations STRL-H.

When entered at EXP2A, this code will print the circular prompt message, until 3 characters have been input. In this case we will simply display the input on the screen. To do this, we will have to have two display areas in use concurrently, since the prompt message needs its own special display area:

EXP2A:	LDA	#0	;clear the	A9	00	
	JSR	CLRDA	;whole screen.	20	lo	hi
	LDA	#10	;get display area	A9	0A	
	JSR	RDAP	;10 parameters.	20	lo	hi
	JSR	PSHZM	;store parameters	20	lo	hi
	EQB	CCN,$3F	;and current display	22	3F	
	JSR	PSHZM	;information on	20	lo	hi
	EQB	DHL,$FF	;the user stack.	28	FF	
	LDA	#1	;get display area 1	A9	01	
	JSR	RDAP	;into the current	20	lo	hi
	LDX	#13	;display area	A2	0D	
EXP2B:	LDA	CCN,X	;and store	B5	22	
	PHA		;it all	48		
	DEX		;on the	CA		
	BPL	EXP2B	;processor stack.	10	FA	
	LDY	#3	;input char count.	A0	03	
	SEC		;set carry for string	38		
EXP2C:	JSR	PULZM	;start and recover	20	lo	hi
	EQB	DHL,$FF	;display area 10	28	FF	
	JSR	PULZM	;parameters and inf	20	lo	hi
	EQB	CCN,$3F	;from user stack.	22	3F	
	LDA	#1	;get prompt message	A9	01	
	JSR	PRMPT	;no., display prompt.	20	lo	hi
	JSR	PSHZM	;after input, store	20	lo	hi
	EQB	CCN,$3F	;updated display inf	22	3F	
	JSR	PSHZM	;and current area on	20	lo	hi
	EQB	DHL,$FF	;the user stack.	28	FF	
	LDX	#0	;recover display	A2	00	
EXP2D:	PLA		;area 1	68		
	STA	CCN,X	;and current	95	22	
	INX		;information	E8		

```
          CPX   #14        ;from the              E0   0E
          BNE   EXP2D      ;processor stack.      D0   F8
          LDA   KCH        ;move input char to    A5   10
          STA   PCH        print location and     85   11
          JSR   PSLCT      ;display it on screen.  20   lo   hi
          DEX              ;makes X = 13           CA
EXP2E:    LDA   CCN,X      ;to store the           B5   22
          PHA              ;updated display        48
          DEX              ;area 1 on the          CA
          BPL   EXP2E      ;processor stack.       10   FA
          CLC              ;to continue prompting. 18
          DEY              ;adjust the count and   88
          BNE   EXP2C      ;get next input char.   D0   CB
          CLD              ;restore                D8
          TSX              ;processor              BA
          TXA              ;stack by               8A
          ADC   #14        ;adding 14 to           69   0E
          TAX              ;the stack              AA
          TXS              ;pointer.               9A
          JSR   ADCZI      ;add 14 to the user     20   lo   hi
          EQB   USPL,$0E   ;stack pointer.         00   0E
          JSR   DL1S       ;delay 1 second.        20   lo   hi
          JMP   ($FFFC)    ;jump to restart.       6C   FC   FF
```

Note how we do not have to bother saving registers in this main code, because we can rely on our utility routines returning them to us unchanged.

PROMPT, MATCH and WARN

PRMPT's ability to display either from the start of a message whose number is in the A register or from the prompt break-off information in page zero locations PRAL-H, PRT and PRF, enables it, in fact, to handle two messages: one asking for input and another warning if incorrect input is given. If the break-off information area in page zero is used instead to point to the incorrect input warning message, the display switches back automatically to the original prompt message when the warning ends.

The requirements of this next piece of code are the same as for EXP2A except that 14 fewer bytes of the user stack are needed. Also, display area 1 will not be used, the routine MATCH from Chapter 7 will be used and DL1S will not, an array number 0, holding the characters you want to be accepted, must be set up and message string 1 will not be used but we will have these messages 2 and 3 instead:

    02   46Choose%what%you%want%to%do%now%by%
            typing%in%the%appropriate%letter.%%%
    03   57%%****%%You%have%asked%for%an%option%
            which%is%not%available.%%Please%try%again.%%
            ****%%

When the code is executed, the circular prompt message will be displayed until a character is given from the keyboard. If this is a character in array 0, it will be in page zero location KCH and its position in the array will be in the A register as the message ends and the screen is cleared. If the character is not in the array, the display switches to message 3 and, if there is no more input before it ends, back to message 2.

EXP3A:	LDA	#0	;clear the	A9	00	
	JSR	CLRDA	;whole screen.	20	lo	hi
	LDA	#10	;make display area	A9	0A	
	JSR	RDAP	;10 params current.	20	lo	hi
	SEC		;set for string start.	38		
EXP3B:	LDA	#2	;get prompt string no.	A9	02	
	JSR	PRMPT	;display prompt messg.	20	lo	hi
	LDY	#0	;now input received,	A0	00	
	LDA	(STRL),Y	;save string 0 char	B1	1C	
	PHA		;count and	48		
	INY		;string first	C8		
	LDA	(STRL),Y	;character	B1	1C	
	PHA		;and	48		
	LDA	KCH	;after getting input,	A5	10	
	STA	(STRL),Y	;replace it	91	1C	
	DEY		;with character	88		
	LDA	#1	;input and string	A9	01	
	STA	(STRL),Y	;count of 1.	91	1C	
	LDY	#0	;get array number	A0	00	
	LDX	#0	;and string number	A2	00	
	JSR	MATCH	;and match them.	20	lo	hi
	TAX		;save input position.	AA		
	PLA		;replace	68		
	INY		;string 0	C8		
	STA	(STRL),Y	;first	91	1C	
	DEY		;character	88		
	PLA		;and	68		
	STA	(STRL),Y	;character count.	91	1C	
	TXA		;recover input pos.	8A		

	BNE	VALID	;branch if matched.	D0	12	
	LDA	#03	;else get invalid	A9	03	
	JSR	STRNG	;message information	20	lo	hi
	JSR	TFRZZ	;moved from user A,	20	lo	hi
	EQB	UAL,PRAL	;UBL(to) UBH(from)	08	14	
	JSR	TFRZZ	;to page zero prompt	20	lo	hi
	EQB	UBL,PRT	;information area.	0A	16	
	CLC		;clear to continue	18		
	BCC	EXP3B	;messg from break-off.	90	C4	
VALID:	JSR	CLCDA	;clear screen and	20	lo	hi
	JMP	($FFFC)	;jump to restart.	6C	FC	FF

Chapter Nine
Conversion

Although the 6502 processor will perform arithmetic operations on Binary Coded Decimal data when the Decimal Mode flag is set, it cannot convert binary data to BCD, or vice versa. To do that, as well as other conversions, you have to write special conversion routines.

Conversion between binary and BCD can be complex because of the different ways in which data can be held – single byte values, double byte values or values held in variable length data fields. The amount of storage space required to hold the converted data is different from the amount needed for the original data. For example, a 16-bit binary number is stored in exactly two bytes but the BCD equivalent needs two and a half bytes.

The two binary-BCD conversion routines in this chapter show the normal conversion techniques – decimal multiplication by 2 when converting to BCD (see Fig. 9.1) and binary multiplication by 10 in the conversion from BCD to binary (see Fig. 9.2).

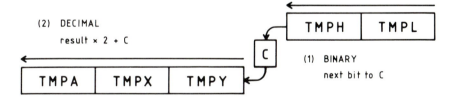

Fig. 9.1. Binary to BCD conversion.

BTBCD – 16-bit binary to 5-digit BCD conversion
Subroutines – STTMP.
Length – 38.
Stack – 3.
Input – X and Y hold a 16-bit binary number (0 to 65535).
Output – 5-digit packed BCD in A, X and Y. D flag set.
Registers changed – P A X Y, TMPL-H-A-P-Y-X.

Method – A loop iterating 16 times multiplies the partial result by 2 using decimal addition and adds the next binary digit (bit). As the highest value of the resulting high order digit cannot exceed 6, decimal addition is not used for this digit multiplication.

BTBCD	SED		;set decimal mode.	F8		
	STY	TMPL	;put binary value in	84	02	
	STX	TMPH	;TMPL-H for bit shifts.	86	03	
	LDA	#0	;zeroise result regs.	A9	00	
	TAX		;TMPA-X-Y on call	AA		
	TAY		;to STTMP.	A8		
	JSR	STTMP	;and save P.	20	lo	hi
	LDY	#16	;16-bit binary count.	A0	10	
BTDLP	ASL	TMPL	;shift next bit out	06	02	
	ROL	TMPH	;into carry.	26	03	
	LDA	TMPY	;decimal multiply	A5	06	
	ADC	TMPY	;partial result by 2	65	06	
	STA	TMPY	;also adding in the	85	06	
	LDA	TMPX	;carry bit out of	A5	07	
	ADC	TMPX	;binary value.	65	07	
	STA	TMPX	;simple shift suffices	85	07	
	ROL	TMPA	;for high digit.	26	04	
	DEY		;repeat for all bits	88		
	BNE	BTDLP	;of binary value.	D0	EB	
	JMP	LDTMP	;return with result.	4C	lo	hi

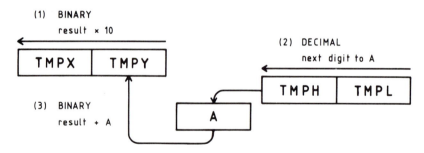

Fig. 9.2. BCD to binary conversion.

BCDTB – 5-digit BCD to 16-bit binary conversion
Subroutines – STTMP.
Length – 62.
Stack – 3.
Input – 5-digit packed BCD in A, X and Y (0 to 65535).
Output – Binary representation in X and Y. D flag reset.
Registers changed – P A X Y, TMPL-H-A-P-Y-X.

Method – The partial result is initialised to the high order digit. Then for each of the remaining four digits: the partial result is multiplied by 10, an inner loop shifts the next digit into A, the digit is added to the partial result. Instead of using a counter for the inner loop, A is initialised to $E0 and this ensures a set carry for 3 iterations and a reset carry on the 4th when the loop ends.

BCDTB	CLD		;binary mode.	D8	
	STY	TMPL	;put low 4 digits in	84	02
	STX	TMPH	;TMPL-H for digit shift.	86	03
	TAY		;init. partial result	A8	
	LDX	#0	;with high digit in	A2	00
	JSR	STTMP	;TMPX-Y and save P.	20	lo hi
	LDY	#4	;4-digit decimal count.	A0	04
DTBLP	LDA	TMPY	;pick up part result in	A5	06
	LDX	TMPX	;X and A, then using	A6	07
	ASL	TMPY	;left shifts and rotates	06	06
	ROL	TMPX	;multiply part result	26	07
	ASL	TMPY	;by 4.	06	06
	ROL	TMPX	;	26	07
	CLC		;now add back	18	
	ADC	TMPY	;picked up part result	65	06
	STA	TMPY	;to give 5 × part	85	06
	TXA		;result in TMPX-Y.	8A	
	ADC	TMPX	;	65	07
	STA	TMPX	;one further 16-bit	85	07
	ASL	TMPY	;shift gives partial	06	06
	ROL	TMPX	;result × 10.	26	07
	LDA	#$E0	;go into loop to shift	A9	E0
DTBND	ASL	TMPL	;next digit into A.	06	02
	ROL	TMPH	;loop ends when set bits	26	03
	ROL	A	;are cleared from A and	2A	
	BCS	DTBND	;reset bit shifts out.	B0	F9
	ADC	TMPY	;add shifted digit in	65	06
	STA	TMPY	;to partial result	85	06
	BCC	DTBLT	;with any carry in	90	02
	INC	TMPX	;to hi-byte.	E6	07
DTBLT	DEY		;repeat for 4 decimal	88	
	BNE	DTBLP	;digits in TMPH-L.	D0	D2
	JMP	LDTMP	;return with result.	4C	lo hi

The remaining two subroutines in this chapter show how you can convert between BCD and ASCII decimal. If you need to convert between binary and ASCII decimal you can use BCD as a 'halfway-house'.

ATBCD – ASCII decimal to packed BCD conversion
Subroutines – None.
Length – 16.
Stack – 1.
Input – 2 ASCII decimal digits in X and Y.
Output – 2 packed BCD digits in A.
Registers changed – P A X.
Method – Stack is used for temporary storage of the first digit. The stack is then indexed by X for combining the two digits in A.

ATBCD	TXA		;get 1st ASCII digit	8A		
	ASL	A	;shift digit part to	0A		
	ASL	A	;hi-nib A, stripping	0A		
	ASL	A	;ASCII hi-nib code at	0A		
	ASL	A	;same time, then store	0A		
	PHA		;on stack. Get 2nd	48		
	TYA		;ASCII digit and strip	98		
	AND	#$0F	;hi-nib code.	29	0F	
	TSX		;index stack to combine	BA		
	ORA	$0101,X	;1st with 2nd digit as	1D	01	01
	INX		;packed BCD. Adjust	E8		
	TXS		;stack to remove stored	9A		
	RTS		;1st digit. Return.	60		

BCDTA – Packed BCD to ASCII decimal conversion
Subroutines – None.
Length – 15.
Stack – 0.
Input – 2 packed BCD digits in A.
Output – 2 ASCII decimal digits in X and Y.
Registers changed – P A X Y.
Method – Each digit has the ASCII hi-nibble code $3 appended.

BCDTA	TAY		;save BCD in Y.	A8	
	LSR	A	;shift 1st digit from	4A	
	LSR	A	;hi-nib A to lo-nib A	4A	
	LSR	A	;leaving high 4 bits	4A	
	LSR	A	;clear, then append	4A	
	ORA	#$30	;ASCII hi-nib code	09	30
	TAX		;and move it to X.	AA	
	TYA		;get 2nd digit back,	98	
	AND	#$0F	;clear high 4 bits,	29	0F
	ORA	#$30	;append ASCII hi-nib	09	30
	TAY		;code and move to Y.	A8	
	RTS		;return.	60	

Chapter Ten
Calculator Program

The routines in this chapter form a complete program which can turn your computer into a 4-register, 8-function, 255-digit, integer calculator. The program is completely self-contained except that it requires a GETCH routine to input ASCII characters from the keyboard. The program has three levels:

● *Top level*. This deals with input commands, ensuring that the correct action is performed. All the logic, including initialisation, is contained in the 193-byte routine CALC. Before using CALC, you do have to put the register addresses in page zero locations UAL to UDH and the register digit length in AML and clear the screen.
● *Middle level*. Three routines – CALCA/CALCS at 58 bytes, CALCM at 65 bytes and CALCD at 67 bytes – perform $+, -, \times, \div$ operations on signed numbers in specific registers.
● *Deepest level*. A set of eight short subroutines perform unsigned arithmetic, digit rotation, clearing, exchange and transfer on registers indirectly indexed by X and A. These routines use the TEMP storage at locations $02 to $07 and have a common subroutine RSTP to deal with this storage. Technically, RSTP is at a fourth level of subroutine nesting. The eight subroutines also share a common exit via REXIT and so they are grouped together as ROSET.

Before using the calculator program, you must put the address of your display line 2, left-most byte, in UAH-L, line 4 address in UBH-L, line 6 address in UCH-L and line 8 address in UDH-L. You must also put the digit-length you require in AML at $3F (AMO and AMW at $3D and $3E are also used by the program but CALC initialises these). The digit-length can be anything from 1 to 255 in theory but must be at most 1 less than your screen width. Register allocation is:

A (line 2) Accumulator = display register.
B (line 4) Secondary register.

C (line 6)   Overflow and remainder register.
D (line 8)   Memory register.

After clearing the screen you can execute CALC which will accept these key inputs:

0 to **9**	Shift digit into A register.
+,−,*,/	Operator between first and second number typed in.
=	After second number to produce result in A with overflow or remainder in C.
#	Change sign in A.
LB, LC, LD	Load A from register B, C or D.
SB, SC, SD	Store A in register B, C or D.
XB, XC, XD	Exchange A with register B, C or D.
Z	Clear E (Error) block after attempted division by zero.
?	End calculator program and return to program which called CALC.

This program does depend on your computer using ASCII codes. If other codes are used then you will have to write the correct codes in CCTAB and in various parts of CALC. Also, the routines in ROSET will have to be changed; the 4th instruction in RADD and the 3rd in RINC ensure that the high nibble of A is either 9 or 0 after the following ADC instruction.

CALC – On screen integer calculator
Subroutines – GETCH (keyboard input in A), CALCA/CALCS, CALCM, CALCD, ROSET.
Length – 193 + 19-byte look-up table.
Stack – 7 plus GETCH stack in excess of 4.
Input – Register addresses in UAH-L, UBH-L, UCH-L and UDH-L.
   Registers digit-length in AML.
   Keyboard input during execution.
Output – During execution, calculations performed on registers.
Registers changed – P A X Y.
Method – The routine loops, inputting commands from the keyboard which are validated against a table – this process also converting the command characters to sequential numbers. Branching occurs to appropriate parts of the routine.

;initialise calculator registers and 'flag' bytes.

CALC	CLD		;ensure binary in CALC.	D8		
	LDY	AML	;digit-length in Y.	A4	3F	
	LDX	#8	;index 'register' A	A2	08	
CCIL	JSR	RCLR	;clear register to	20	lo	hi

	INX		;zeros with '+' sign	E8	
	INX		;index next register	E8	
	CPX	#16	;repeat for 'registers'	E0	10
	BNE	CCIL	;A, B, C and D.	D0	F7
	LDA	#0	;clear operator byte	A9	00
	STA	AMO	;in AMO and set input	85	3D
	STA	AMW	;digit to new number.	85	3E

;validate input command, converted to a number.

CCLP	JSR	GETCH	;get key-in in A	20	lo	hi
	LDX	#19	;index table end byte	A2	13	
CCGLP	CMP	CCTAB,X	;loop till input	DD	lo	hi
	BEQ	CCVCH	;matches or	F0	05	
	DEX		;X goes past start	CA		
	BPL	CCGLP	;of valid table when	10	F8	
	BMI	CCLP	;go get new input.	30	F1	
CCVCH	TXA		;command number to A	8A		
	LDX	#8	;index 'register' A	A2	08	

;test for sign change command '#', new no. 10.

	CMP	#10	;branch if	C9	0A
	BNE	CCNSC	;not sign change A.	D0	08
	LDA	(0,X)	;get sign byte, change	A1	00
	EOR	#%00000110	;+ to −, or − to +,	49	06
	STA	(0,X)	;replace it and	81	00
	BNE	CCLP	;get next command.	D0	E2

;test for digits, new nos. 0 to 9. Shift digit in.

CCNSC	BCS	CCND	;branch if > 9 on flag	B0	13	
	ORA	#$30	;from last CMP. Put in	09	30	
	INC	AMW	;ASCII hi-nib. Test for	E6	3E	
	BEQ	CCDOK	;okay to shift or first	F0	03	
	JSR	RCLR	;clear for new number.	20	lo	hi
CCDOK	JSR	RRLD	;feed digit in from	20	lo	hi
	LDA	#−1	;right. Flag current no.	A9	FF	
CCAMW	STA	AMW	;set/reset new no. flag	85	3E	
	DEX		;in AMW. Ensure branch	CA		
	BNE	CCLP	;to get next command.	D0	CD	

;test register move. Get register name.

CCND	SBC	#14	;X, S and L below zero	E9	0E	
	BCS	CCNSW	;branch if >= 0.	B0	25	
	CMP	#−2	;test X, S or L and	C9	FE	
	PHP		;save result while	08		
CCSLP	JSR	GETCH	;getting register name.	20	lo	hi
	CMP	"E"	;loop till B, C or D	C9	45	
	BCS	CCSLP	;is input.	B0	F9	
	CMP	"B"	;	C9	42	
	BCC	CCSLP	;	90	F5	

	SBC	#61	;convert ASCII code to	E9	3D	
	ASL	A	;register address index.	0A		
	PLP		;get X, S or L flags	28		
	BCS	CCNX	;skip if not exchange	B0	05	
	JSR	REXG	;else (X) exchange (A).	20	lo	hi
	BNE	CCWZ	;	D0	08	
CCNX	BNE	CCNS	;skip if not store	D0	03	
	TAX		;else swap pointers.	AA		
	LDA	#8	;	A9	08	
CCNS	JSR	RTFR	;move (A) to (X).	20	lo	hi
CCWZ	LDA	#0	;flag for new no.	A9	00	
	BEQ	CCAMW	;go store in AMW.	F0	D2	
;test operators =, +, −, *, /. Now numbers 0 to 4.						
CCNSW	CMP	#5	;skip if not operator	C9	05	
	BEQ	CCEND	;so must be '?', end.	F0	4C	
	PHA		;save this operator.	48		
	LDA	AMO	;test last operator	A5	3D	
	BEQ	CCBCL	;skip if '='.	F0	36	
	LDA	#10	;exchange registers for	A9	0A	
	JSR	REXG	;(A) operation (B).	20	lo	hi
	DEC	AMO	;skip if last operator	C6	3D	
	BNE	CCST	;not '+'.	D0	03	
	JSR	CALCA	;else do (A) + (B).	20	lo	hi
CCST	DEC	AMO	;skip if operator	C6	3D	
	BNE	CCMT	;not '−'.	D0	03	
	JSR	CALCS	;else do (A) − (B).	20	lo	hi
CCMT	DEC	AMO	;skip if operator	C6	3D	
	BNE	CCDT	;not '*'.	D0	03	
	JSR	CALCM	;else do (A)×(B).	20	lo	hi
CCDT	DEC	AMO	;skip if operator	C6	3D	
	BNE	CCBCL	;not '/'.	D0	18	
	JSR	CALCD	;else do (A) / (B).	20	lo	hi
	BCC	CCBCL	;skip if not division	90	13	
	LDX	#8	;by zero, else clear	A2	08	
	JSR	RCLR	;register A and write	20	lo	hi
	LDA	"E"	;'E' for Error block	A9	45	
	STA	(UAL),Y	;in register A.	91	08	
CCZLP	JSR	GETCH	;loop till 'Z' input	20	lo	hi
	CMP	"Z"	;to clear block	C9	5A	
	BNE	CCZLP	;then clear 'E' from	D0	F9	
	JSR	RCLR	;register A, continue	20	lo	hi
CCBCL	LDX	#10	;clear register B at	A2	0A	
	JSR	RCLR	;end of operation.	20	lo	hi
	PLA		;recover new operator	68		
	STA	AMO	;and store for next time	85	3D	

	BEQ	CCWZ	;skip if '=' to flag a	F0	B3	
	LDA	#8	;new no. else move	A9	08	
	JSR	RTFR	;'Accumulator' to	20	lo	hi
	BNE	CCWZ	;secondary register.	D0	AC	
CCEND	RTS		;exit if '?' input.	60		

;valid input table – character to sequential number.

CCTAB	EQB	48,49,50	;0, 1, 2,	30	31	32
	EQB	51,52,53	;3, 4, 5,	33	34	35
	EQB	54,55,56	;6, 7, 8,	36	37	38
	EQB	57,35,88	;9, #, X,	39	23	58
	EQB	83,76,61	;S, L, =,	53	4C	3D
	EQB	43,45,42	;+, −, *,	2B	2D	2A
	EQB	47,63	;/, ?	2F	3F	

CALCA, CALCS – ASCII multibyte addition, subtraction

Subroutines – ROSET.

Length – 58.

Stack – 4.

Input – UAH-L and UBH-L address the sign bytes of the two arguments. AML contains the digit length.

Output – Result addressed by UAH-L, overflow by UCH-L.

Registers changed – P A X Y.

Method – The argument signs are tested to determine whether addition or subtraction of the magnitudes should take place. Overflow from addition is stored in the argument addressed by UCH-L. If subtraction results in going below zero then the result is negated and the sign changed.

CALCA	LDA	#0	;CALCA split is exact	A9	00	
	BEQ	CASC	;opposite of CALCS	F0	02	
CALCS	LDA	#6	;split on sign test.	A9	06	
	LDX	#12	;index overflow	A2	0C	
	JSR	RCLR	;and clear it.	20	lo	hi
	LDX	#8	;index 1st argument.	A2	08	
	LDY	AML	;digit-length to Y.	A4	3F	
	EOR	(0,X)	;exclusive-or add/sub	41	00	
	EOR	(2,X)	;bits with sign bytes	41	02	
	BNE	CASS	;to determine subtract	D0	0E	
	LDA	#10	;or add. Index 2nd	A9	0A	
	JSR	RADD	;argument and add	20	lo	hi
	BCC	CASND	;magnitudes	90	17	
	LDX	#12	;with any overflow to	A2	0C	
	JSR	RINC	;overflow argument.	20	lo	hi
	BNE	CASND	;	D0	10	

CASS	LDA	#10	;do sub. Index 2nd	A9	0A	
	JSR	RSUB	;argument and subtract	20	lo	hi
	BCS	CASND	;magnitudes. If gone	B0	09	
	JSR	RNEG	;below zero negate it,	20	lo	hi
	LDA	(0,X)	;get sign byte, change	A1	00	
	EOR	#%00000110	;+ to −, or − to +,	49	06	
	STA	(0,X)	;and replace it.	81	00	
CASND	LDX	#8	;finally, copy	A2	08	
	LDA	(0,X)	;result sign to	A1	00	
	STA	(4,X)	;overflow arg. sign	81	04	
	RTS		;and return.	60		

CALCM – ASCII multibyte multiplication
Subroutines – ROSET.
Length – 65.
Stack – 4.
Input – UAH-L and UBH-L address the sign bytes of the two arguments. AML contains the digit length.
Output – Product addressed by UAH-L, overflow by UCH-L.
Registers changed – P A X Y.
Method – Long multiplication by shifting and multiple addition at the correct place. Product sign is obtained by exclusive-oring the argument signs.

CALCM	LDX	#8	;Index 1st argument and	A2	08	
	LDA	#12	;overflow. Move 1st into	A9	0C	
	JSR	REXG	;overflow for digit shift	20	lo	hi
	JSR	RCLR	;out, clear 1st for	20	lo	hi
	LDY	AML	;product. Get length.	A4	3F	
CMLP	LDA	"0"	;shift partial product	A9	30	
	JSR	RRLD	;by one digit, moving	20	lo	hi
	LDX	#12	;next multiplier digit	A2	0C	
	JSR	RRLD	;out into A and strip	20	lo	hi
	LDX	#8	;it of ASCII hi-nibble	A2	08	
	AND	#$0F	;by AND. Skip if it is	29	0F	
	BEQ	CMLPT	;zero else store in AMW	F0	14	
	STA	AMW	;as multiple add count.	85	3E	
	LDA	#10	;index multiplicand	A9	0A	
CMALP	JSR	RADD	;add to partial product	20	lo	hi
	BCC	CMALT	;with any carry over	90	07	
	LDX	#12	;into overflow	A2	0C	
	JSR	RINC	;looping for as	20	lo	hi
	LDX	#8	;many times as value	A2	08	
CMALT	DEC	AMW	;of current multiplier	C6	3E	

	BNE	CMALP	;digit in AMW.	D0	F0	
CMLPT	DEC	AML	;repeat for all	C6	3F	
	BNE	CMLP	;multiplier digits.	D0	D8	
	STY	AML	;restore AML from Y.	84	3F	
	LDA	(2,X)	;get product sign '+'	A1	02	
	EOR	(4,X)	;if argument signs same,	41	04	
	EOR	"+"	;or '—' if different,	49	2B	
	STA	(0,X)	;into product sign	81	00	
	STA	(4,X)	;and overflow sign.	81	04	
	RTS		;return.	60		

CALCD – ASCII multibyte division

Subroutines – ROSET.

Length – 67.

Stack – 4.

Input – UAH-L and UBH-L address the sign bytes of the two arguments. AML contains the digit length.

Output – Carry set: attempted division by zero – no change. Carry reset: quotient addressed by UAH-L, remainder addressed by UCH-L.

Registers changed – P A X Y.

Method – Long division by shifting and multiple subtraction giving individual quotient digits at correct place.

CALCD	LDX	#10	;index divisor and test	A2	0A	
	JSR	RNEG	;for zero by negating	20	lo	hi
	JSR	RNEG	;twice leaving value	20	lo	hi
	BCS	CDEND	;unchanged but C reset	B0	38	
	LDX	#12	;only if okay. Clear	A2	0C	
	JSR	RCLR	;for remainder and	20	lo	hi
	LDY	AML	;pick up digit length.	A4	3F	
CDLP	LDA	"0"	;zeroise next place	A9	30	
	STA	AMW	;digit in AMW. Shift	85	3E	
	LDX	#8	;partial quotient in and	A2	08	
	JSR	RRLD	;dividend digit into	20	lo	hi
	LDX	#12	;remainder for next	A2	0C	
	JSR	RRLD	;place subtraction.	20	lo	hi
	LDA	#10	;index divisor then	A9	0A	
CDSLP	JSR	RSUB	;loop, subtracting	20	lo	hi
	INC	AMW	;divisor and adding 1	E6	3E	
	BCS	CDSLP	;to next quotient digit	B0	F9	
	JSR	RADD	;until negative result	20	lo	hi
	DEC	AMW	;so add back and correct	C6	3E	
	LDA	AMW	;next digit, pick it up	A5	3E	

	STA	(UAL),Y	;in A and put to end of	91	08
	DEC	AML	;quotient. Repeat for	C6	3F
	BNE	CDLP	;all dividend digits.	D0	DC
	STY	AML	;restore AML from Y.	84	3F
	LDA	(−4,X)	;get dividend sign to	A1	FC
	STA	(0,X)	;remainder. Quotient	81	00
	EOR	(−2,X)	;sign calculated from	41	FE
	EOR	"+"	;argument signs into	49	2B
	STA	(−4,X)	;quotient. Clear carry	81	FC
	CLC		;to show division done.	18	
CDEND	RTS		;return.	60	

ROSET – ASCII register operations set, incorporating RCLR, REXG, RTFR, RRLD, RADD, RSUB, RNEG and RINC

Subroutines – RSTP, local within ROSET to move pointers into TEMP store, save X and Y in TEMP store and set D for decimal arithmetic.

Length – 174 in total.

Stack – 2 for each incorporated routine.

Input – X indexes page zero location of address of 1st argument. A either indexes for 2nd argument (REXG, RTFR, RADD, RSUB) or contains new digit (RRLD) or is not used (RCLR, RNEG, RINC). Y contains digit-length.

Output – see individual entry points.

Registers changed – P (also A in RRLD).

Method – Each incorporated routine calls RSTP to move addresses to TEMP store and save X and Y in TEMP store. Individual actions are performed, then each exits via REXIT to restore register values and clear Decimal flag.

;RSTP – Store parameters. 25 bytes.

RSTP	STX	TMPX	;put X and Y to TEMP	86	07
	STY	TMPY	;then move address in	84	06
	LDY	0,X	;location indexed by X	B4	00
	STY	TMPL	;into TMPL-H. This is	84	02
	LDY	1,X	;the address of the 1st	B4	01
	STY	TMPH	;or only argument.	84	03
	TAX		;get possible index	AA	
	LDY	0,X	;from A into X and put	B4	00
	STY	TMPA	;2nd argument address	84	04
	LDY	1,X	;into TMPA-P.	B4	01
	STY	TMPP	;	84	05
	LDY	TMPY	;recover length to Y.	A4	06
	SED		;set for decimal maths	F8	

	RTS		;return.	60		

;RCLR – clear register, sign positive. 16 bytes.

RCLR	JSR	RSTP	;initialise.	20	lo	hi
	LDA	"0"	;ASCII zero to A and	A9	30	
RCLRL	STA	(TMPL),Y	;to all digits in 1st	91	02	
	DEY		;argument.	88		
	BNE	RCLRL	;	D0	FB	
	LDA	"+"	;positive sign into	A9	2B	
	STA	(TMPL),Y	;sign byte.	91	02	
	BNE	REXIT	;restore and return.	D0	7E	

;REXG – exchange registers, byte for byte. 20 bytes.

REXG	JSR	RSTP	;initialise.	20	lo	hi
REXGL	LDA	(TMPL),Y	;get byte from 1st	B1	02	
	PHA		;argument and save on	48		
	LDA	(TMPA),Y	;stack while moving in	B1	04	
	STA	(TMPL),Y	;byte from 2nd to 1st.	91	02	
	PLA		;recover stored byte and	68		
	STA	(TMPA),Y	;put into 2nd arg.	91	04	
	DEY		;repeat for all bytes	88		
	CPY	#−1	;including sign bytes	C0	FF	
	BNE	REXGL	;at index zero.	D0	F1	
	BEQ	REXIT	;restore and return.	F0	6A	

;RTFR – transfer 2nd register to 1st. 14 bytes.

RTFR	JSR	RSTP	;initialise.	20	lo	hi
RTFRL	LDA	(TMPA),Y	;move byte from 2nd to	B1	04	
	STA	(TMPL),Y	;1st argument.	91	02	
	DEY		;repeat for all bytes	88		
	CPY	#−1	;including sign byte	C0	FF	
	BNE	RTFRL	;at index zero.	D0	F7	
	BEQ	REXIT	;restore and return.	F0	5C	

;RRLD – rotate register left through A by one digit. Output
;A holds high order digit shifted out. 16 bytes.

RRLD	JSR	RSTP	;initialise.	20	lo	hi
RRLDL	PHA		;save shift in digit	48		
	LDA	(TMPL),Y	;get shift out digit	B1	02	
	TAX		;to X. Recover shift in	AA		
	PLA		;digit and put into	68		
	STA	(TMPL),Y	;argument. Move shift	91	02	
	TXA		;out digit to A as next	8A		
	DEY		;shift in digit. Repeat	88		
	BNE	RRLDL	;for all digits.	D0	F5	
	BEQ	REXIT	;restore and return.	F0	4C	

;RADD – add 2nd register to 1st (unsigned). Carry set if
;overflow. 21 bytes.

RADD	JSR	RSTP	;initialise.	20	lo	hi

	CLC		;no carry in.	18		
RADDL	LDA	(TMPL),Y	;get digit, make hi-nib	B1	02	
	EOR	#%01010000	;= %0110 so on addition	49	50	
	ADC	(TMPA),Y	;any carry goes straight	71	04	
	AND	#$0F	;through hi-nib to C.	29	0F	
	ORA	#$30	;ensure ASCII hi-nib in	09	30	
	STA	(TMPL),Y	;result is correct.	91	02	
	DEY		;repeat for	88		
	BNE	RADDL	;all digits.	D0	F1	
	BEQ	REXIT	;restore and return.	F0	37	

;RSUB – subtract 2nd register from 1st. On output, C is 1
;if subtraction has gone okay, else C = 0 for gone below
;zero. Unsigned subtraction. 19 bytes.

RSUB	JSR	RSTP	;initialise.	20	lo	hi
	SEC		;no borrow initially.	38		
RSUBL	LDA	(TMPL),Y	;subtract 2nd argument	B1	02	
	SBC	(TMPA),Y	;byte from 1st in A	F1	04	
	AND	#$0F	;then ensure ASCII	29	0F	
	ORA	#$30	;digit hi-nib code	09	30	
	STA	(TMPL),Y	;and put in result	91	02	
	DEY		;repeat for all	88		
	BNE	RSUBL	;digits.	D0	F3	
	BEQ	REXIT	;restore and return.	F0	24	

;RNEG – negate (10's complement) register, ignoring sign
;byte. Output C = 0 unless argument = 0. 19 bytes.

RNEG	JSR	RSTP	;initialise.	20	lo	hi
	SEC		;no borrow initially.	38		
RNEGL	LDA	"0"	;subtract argument byte	A9	30	
	SBC	(TMPL),Y	;from ASCII zero then	F1	02	
	AND	#$0F	;ensure result is an	29	0F	
	ORA	#$30	;ASCII digit before	09	30	
	STA	(TMPL),Y	;restoring to argument.	91	02	
	DEY		;repeat for all digits	88		
	BNE	RNEGL	;of argument.	D0	F3	
	BEQ	REXIT	;restore and return.	F0	11	

;RINC – increment register magnitude. C = 1 on overflow.
;17 bytes.

RINC	JSR	RSTP	;initialise.	20	lo	hi
	SEC		;C = 1 for add 1.	38		
RINCL	LDA	#$60	;ensure any carry from	A9	60	
	ADC	(TMPL),Y	;addition of 0 to byte	71	02	
	AND	#$0F	;goes through hi-nib	29	0F	
	ORA	#$30	;into C. Ensure ASCII	09	30	
	STA	(TMPL),Y	;digit result.	91	02	
	DEY		;repeat for all digits	88		

```
          BNE    RINCL      ;of argument, then ...   D0   F3
;REXIT – common exit for all routines. Restore register
;contents and clear Decimal flag. 7 bytes.
REXIT    TXA               ;restore A from X,        8A
         LDX    TMPX       ;X and Y from TEMP        A6   07
         LDY    TMPY       ;store, resetting Z       A4   06
         CLD               ;since Y > 0. Clear       D8
         RTS               ;decimal mode. Return.    60
```

Chapter Eleven
Relocatable Code

The prime consideration in writing the routines in this book has been to ensure that they will work on most computers using the 6502 processor. The routines in Chapters 1 to 9 which are intended as the basic building blocks of any program, or even a complete system, have also been written to be *relocatable*. Relocatable code will operate correctly in any area of memory.

A machine code program or subroutine is tied to a specific area of memory if any part of it is addressed directly. If an instruction is assumed by another part of the program to be at a specific address then it must be at that address or an error will occur in the program. Such a program is *location-specific* and cannot be moved without changing those of its instructions which use direct addresses.

There may be many reasons for wishing to move whole programs or shorter code sequences to different memory locations. We can identify six major needs:

(1) *Portability*. Computer manufacturers appear to dread the prospect of software written for their machines being used on those of their competitors or vice versa, and consequently 'user' RAM rarely occupies the same areas of memory in different computer systems.

(2) *Development*. However much effort goes into program design, there is almost invariably a need to 'shuffle around' sections of the program.

(3) *Debugging*. Insertion of just one accidentally omitted byte could alter the addresses of almost all the program instructions.

(4) *Updating*. Adapting programs to meet changing needs will probably require some shifting about to make room for additions.

(5) *Library routines*. General purpose routines ought ideally to

require no alteration when used at different locations in different programs.

(6) *Multi-program conflict*. In certain situations it may be desirable or necessary to run several programs concurrently (achieved in practice by running a slice of each program in turn) and these programs must be relocatable to avoid location clashes.

All of these needs can be met, of course, by using an editor-assembler which operates on labels rather than absolute addresses. Relocation is simply a matter of re-assembling at a different origin. Wherever and whenever possible we recommend you to use an assembler for machine code programming.

There are occasions when the use of an assembler is not practical. Perhaps the system is tiny, with insufficient memory for an assembler, assembler mnemonic source program and machine code object program. Perhaps the machine code subroutines are included in a BASIC program, or perhaps you don't have an assembler anyway. On these occasions it is wise to consider ways of minimising the use of absolute addresses. A little forethought could save a lot of tedious work later.

The 6502 is less amenable to relocatable code than other popular 8-bit processors. It does not have the relative subroutine call and relative jump of the 6809 nor the register indirect addressing of the Z80. Many of its instructions use the absolute direct or absolute indexed addressing modes which require specific 16-bit addresses written as the second and third instruction bytes.

In code designed to be relocatable, only page 0 (invariably used as a set of 256 pseudo-registers because of the special *zero page* instructions) and page 1 (hard-wired as the 6502 stack) can be addressed directly. Locations from $0200 to $FFFF should be addressed only indirectly using the pre-indexed and post-indexed indirect modes (see Appendix A) which operate on addresses stored in page zero. Addresses used indirectly in this way can be computed by the program; they will be automatically different if the program is relocated. The cost of this attempt at relocatability is an increase in operating time and often a large increase in the length of a program. This is because either the index registers constantly have to be updated or adjustments have to be made continually to the addresses in page zero.

The heaviest use of direct addressing occurs in JMP and JSR instructions. The 6502 instruction set does include an indirect jump instruction which loads the Program Counter with the 16-bit value held at a specified address – which can be in page zero and can be computed rather than programmed. The only program relative jumps, however, are the Branch instructions with maximum jump distances of 128 bytes back or 127 bytes forward from the address next following the Branch offset. All the Branches are conditional on the state of just one of the Negative, Zero, Overflow and Carry flags. There is no indirect, program relative or conditional subroutine call. We shall examine two methods of making programs relocatable even while retaining use of direct JMP and JSR.

Jump tables

This is a method particularly useful during program development when chunks of the program may be constantly shuffled around. The addresses of all JSR and JMP destinations are built into a table of JMP instructions which is external to the program. All jumps and subroutine calls in the program are then routed through the table to the correct destination. Any code relocation changing these destinations does not affect the JSR and JMP instructions – which continue to address the unmoved jump table – but only the easily found addresses in the jump table entries. This can eliminate many tedious searches through the program.

The main disadvantage to the method is that the table itself is fixed – it is *location-specific* – and subject to exactly the same difficulties met by location-specific programs, though to a lesser degree since the table requires only a small area of memory.

A relative jump routine

LBRM and LBRSM provide the 6502 with a program relative jump and subroutine call, both of which are conditional on the status of any combination of flags. Although allowing for greater sophistication in program design, they are slow in operation and turn 3-byte JMP and JSR into 7-byte instructions. Their use is demonstrated by the following code which causes a relative jump only if the Carry and Overflow flags are set and the Zero flag reset:

```
4F21        JSR    LBRM           ;                    20   lo   hi
4F24        EQB    $41,$43        ;state & mask.       41   43
4F26        EQW    DEST – NEXT    ;16-bit offset.      E2   0C
```

4F28 NEXT (next instruction)   ;   .
.   .   .
.   .   .
.   .   .
5C0A DEST (jump destination)   ;   .

The third and fourth byte parameters embedded after the call to
LBRM give the number of bytes between the 7-byte jump and its
destination ($5C0A − $4F28 = $0CE2), not the destination address
($5C0A). The addresses are altered when the program is relocated
but not the distance between them.

A relative jump routine is most useful for effecting internal jumps
in a fully developed and debugged block of interrelated routines
used in different locations as, for example, a block of library
routines in different programs. It is not tied to any one program –
unlike the jump table – and can be fixed in memory for use by all
programs in a multi-program environment.

LBRM & LBRSM – Long branch (subroutine) on flag mask
Subroutines – PARAM, LDTMP.
Length – 54.
Stack – 5.
Input – Four parameters after JSR LBRM/LBRSM.
    P1: selected flags status for test.
    P2: flag mask (bit = 1 = test flag).
    P3,4: lo- and hi-bytes of 16-bit branch offset.
Output – Program relative jump (subroutine call) effected if P1 = P2
    AND status register P. Else immediate return to location following
    parameters.
Registers changed – None.
Method – PARAM is called to get P1 (test status) into X and P2
    (flag mask) into A. The flag mask is logically ANDed with the flag
    register P to isolate those flags to be tested. The test status in X is
    compared to the selected flags. If the two do not match, the
    stacked return address is moved past P3 and P4 and immediate
    return is made (no jump). Else jump or call is to be made so
    PARAM is called to get the offset (P3,4) into X and Y. If LBRM
    entry, the return address is removed from stack. The branch
    destination is computed by adding the offset to the parameter
    address stored in TMPL-H by PARAM, adding 2 to account for
    P3,4 and it is then put on stack for an RTS effected jump.

LBRM	JSR	PARAM	;P1 & P2 into X and A.	20	lo	hi
	LDY	#0	;mark LBRM entry.	A0	00	
	BEQ	LBCMN	;skip to common code.	F0	05	
LBRSM	JSR	PARAM	;P1 & P2 into X and A.	20	lo	hi
	LDY	#1	;mark LBRSM entry.	A0	01	
LBCMN	CLD		;for binary addition.	D8		
	AND	TMPP	;select flags for test,	25	05	
	STA	TMPL	;compare to test byte	85	02	
	CPX	TMPL	;and return to next	E4	02	
	BNE	LBSWD	;instr. if no match.	D0	13	
	DEY		;set Z if LBRSM entry.	88		
	JSR	PARAM+3	;get offset without	20	lo	hi
	BEQ	LBAWD	;storing regs. Remove	F0	02	
	PLA		;return address from	68		
	PLA		;stack if LBRM entry	68		
LBAWD	CLC		;add offset in X and Y	18		
	TXA		;to offset address put	8A		
	ADC	TMPL	;in TMPL-H by PARAM	65	02	
	TAX		;giving destination	AA		
	TYA		;minus 2, put it on	98		
	ADC	TMPH	;stack for increment	65	03	
	PHA		;to account for P3,4.	48		
	TXA		;	8A		
	PHA		;	48		
LBSWD	CLC		;get return address	18		
	PLA		;(or displaced branch	68		
	ADC	#2	;address) incremented	69	02	
	TAX		;to account for P3,4.	AA		
	PLA		;take care of any	68		
	ADC	#0	;carry to hi-byte.	69	00	
	PHA		;put it back on stack	48		
	TXA		;for exit to correct	8A		
	PHA		;address via LDTMP	48		
	JMP	LDTMP	;and restore registers.	4C	lo	hi

Chapter Twelve
Points on Display

Recent microcomputer developments have seen the implementation of dedicated graphics chips and an increasing complexity in the type and amount of information required to use graphics on a memory-mapped display. Because of this, and the fact that any graphics system depends to a great extent on hardware, there are considerable differences between the graphics systems of different computers. However, at the most simple graphics level – that of illuminating individual points on the display – most computers adhere to certain general principles. In this chapter we show how these principles can be applied in three of the most common types of graphics.

Block graphics

'Block graphics' is the name commonly given to a set of predefined and unalterable shapes which may be written to screen in the same way as ordinary alphabetic characters. These shapes are usually given the codes from $80 to $FF. If your computer has block graphics then sending one of these codes to the print routine should result in a shape instead of a letter being printed on the display.

Within the full graphics set you may find a subset of 16 characters which allow you to illuminate any combination of the four quarters of each screen location. These are quite likely to be scattered randomly throughout the full set. Unfortunately, some computer manufacturers have been a little shortsighted in the design of their predefined graphics set. The Ohio Superboard and the Compukit UK 101, for example, both have a wide range of block graphics but neither has a complete set of the 'quarter square pixels'.

The best known computer using block graphics is the Commodore PET and it is the graphics codes used on the PET which we

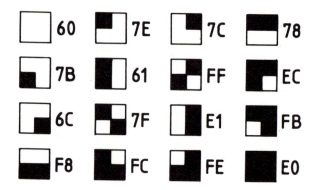

Fig. 12.1. Block graphics quarter squares (PET codes).

use to illustrate the type. Figure 12.1 shows the full set of useful pixel shapes with PET codes, the shaded portions indicating which parts will be lit on the screen.

Quarter square block graphics allows you to plot twice as many points horizontally as characters on a line and twice as many vertical points as lines on the display. Mixing text and graphics is always allowed.

Pixel block

This is similar to the block graphics method except that a complete set of sixty-four characters is used to illuminate any combination of sixths of a screen location. The most common pixel block currently in use is the Teletext system as used in the **BBC Microcomputer** graphics mode 7.

Sixty-four codes in consecutive groupings are used for the characters and they are arranged in such a way that each of six bits of the code byte will illuminate one pixel if it is set. By setting more than one code bit, any of the pixels in the block may be lit at the same time. Figure 12.2 shows which bits have to be set to illuminate each pixel in the Teletext system. Bit 5 of the code is always set and bit 7 may be always set or always reset.

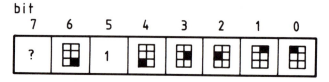

Fig. 12.2. Pixel block (Teletext) pixel selection codes.

The pixel block system allows you to plot twice as many points horizontally as characters on a line and three times as many vertical points as lines on the display. It usually, but not always, lets you mix text with graphics. The Teletext pixel block system requires you to use graphics control codes to switch between text and graphics. You should consult your manual on what these are and how to use them.

High resolution

This, strictly speaking, is the ability to address each individual point of light on your display, although some computers with 'high resolution' allow you only to address small groups of these points.

In the most simple implementation of high resolution graphics, each point is lit or unit by a single bit of data in a screen location being set or reset. Colour complicates matters by requiring several bits to determine if a point is 'on' and, if so, what colour it is. To use the Apple as an example: bits 6 to 0 of each screen location byte illuminate seven horizontally sequential points. Bit 7 (not displayed) is used to select between a violet/green and a blue/red colour set for those seven points. Any illuminated point in an even numbered column on the screen will show as violet or blue; those in odd numbered columns will be green or red. Two adjacent points will appear as white.

The sample high resolution graphics we use in the routine MPLOT assumes each screen location byte to match 8 bits to 8 screen points as in Figure 12.3.

bit:	7	6	5	4	3	2	1	0
dot:	0	1	2	3	4	5	6	7

Fig. 12.3. High resolution dot selection.

It is usual for high resolution graphics to have a different area of video memory from that used for the text screen and so mixing of text and graphics is not common. The resolution, compared to text lines and columns, varies but the number of horizontal points displayed is commonly eight times the number of characters per line and vertical points are eight times the number of lines. The maximum area addressable by the graphics routines in this book is

256 × 256 points which may be less than your high resolution screen in the horizontal direction.

The coordinate system

The most common method of addressing individual pixels or dots on display is by an *x,y* coordinate system with *x* identifying the horizontal displacement from the origin and *y* the vertical.

The position of the origin – coordinate (0, 0) – is not standardised. Some systems use the top left pixel as the origin and some use the bottom left. There is no hardware necessity for the origin to be in any particular location; its position is just a whim of the software writer. To conform to standard mathematical practice, we use the bottom left pixel of the graphics display area as origin in all the graphics routines which use the information in page zero graphics variables at $30 to $3C (see Chapter 3).

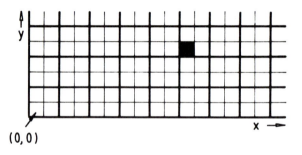

Fig. 12.4. Block graphics pixel at (10, 4).

Figures 12.4 to 12.6 show the lower left part of a graphics display area with one set pixel at (10, 4). Since each screen location byte contains 4, 6 or 8 pixels or dots, the *x* and *y* pixel offsets from the

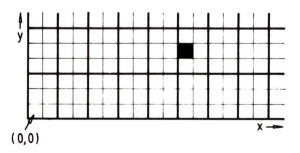

Fig. 12.5. Pixel block pixel at (10, 4).

origin pixel have to be converted into byte of address offsets from the origin byte location. Having ascertained the number of complete bytes in the offset, the *x* and *y* remainders are used to determine the code which will result in the correct pixel being set. The PET code for the quarter square in Figure 12.4 is $7B, the Teletext code for the pixel in Figure 12.5 will be either $24 or $A4 depending on whether bit 7 is usually set or reset. Our sample high resolution code for Figure 12.6 is $20.

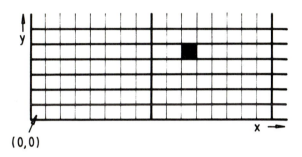

Fig. 12.6. High resolution dot at (10, 4).

The display screen

Using stored variables for the origin address and the high indices of the *x* and *y* offsets (at $30 to $33) means that you do not have to use the whole of your computer's display area. These variables can be changed to suit your needs.

In the CAPTI part of MPLOT we assume that screen locations are addressed sequentially along each row (a difference of 1 byte) and that vertically consecutive locations (running down each column) have equal byte differences. This value is assembled as RDIFF and you will have to insert the value appropriate to your display. Some computers – notably the Apple and the BBC Micro – arrange video memory in blocks so that not all differences are equal. If this is done in your computer then you will have to change parts of CAPTI.

MPLOT structure

MPLOT is written in modules for three reasons. Firstly, it is written to work for three different types of graphics. Alternative versions of some of the modules are given for different graphics types. You need only include the version appropriate to your graphics system. Secondly, computers using the same types of graphics do differ and you may have to change part of MPLOT to suit your system. If this is the case then you will find that possibly only one module has to be changed – far easier than having to rewrite the entire routine. Thirdly, it demonstrates a time and labour-saving method of programming. Splitting any routine up into single-task parts gets the work done faster and without getting into a muddle. The first and second reasons are sufficient justification for the third.

Pixel operations

The LOGIC part of MPLOT accepts 4 modes. The mode must be stored in PLTM at $38 before MPLOT is called.

Mode 2 is the PLOT mode. This results in the addressed pixel being illuminated regardless of its previous state. Mode 3, UNPLOT, ensures that the addressed pixel is cleared. Mode 1, INVERT, is used to produce a change in the state of the addressed pixel.

Mode 0 is the TEST mode. This can be used to determine the current condition of any part of the screen, one pixel at a time. If saving part of a screenful of information, TEST mode can determine which pixels are set so that their coordinates can be saved. The coordinates can then be used later to re-plot the saved screen at the same position or, with an offset, at a different location. If you are adventurous, TEST can be used to help fill in a shape after drawing the outline. Starting from within the shape, each pixel is first tested to see if the boundary has been reached before using PLOT mode to set it.

MPLOT – Modal plot
Subroutines – STTMP, LDTMP. Local modules: CAPTI, RGCBP, LOGIC, WBPGC.
Length – 37 plus modules.
Stack – 3.
Input – x,y coordinates in PLTX,PLTY. Mode in PLTM. Modes: 0 = TEST, 1 = INVERT, 2 = PLOT, 3 = UNPLOT.
Output – Result flagged in PLTR:
   bit 7 reset = out of area – no action.

bit 7 set = action taken, bit 0 reset: point off

bit 0 set: point on.

Registers changed – None.

Method – Top level performs the task of validating the coordinates against the pixels high indices GXN and GYN. Modules are then called to perform the necessary actions. Modules are given for PET block graphics, Teletext pixel block and high resolution.

MPLOT	JSR	STTMP	;save registers in TEMP.	20	lo	hi
	CLD		;for binary arithmetic.	D8		
	LDA	#0	;clear results byte	A9	00	
	STA	PLTR	;before testing if	85	39	
	LDA	GXN	;*x* pixels hi-index is	A5	32	
	CMP	PLTX	;less than *x* coordinate.	C5	34	
	BCC	MPSR	;skip if it is, else	90	04	
	LDA	GYN	;test *y* validity	A5	33	
	CMP	PLTY	;getting	C5	35	
MPSR	ROR	PLTR	;result to bit 7 and	66	39	
	BEQ	MPEND	;end if out of limits.	F0	0C	
	JSR	CAPTI	;address byte location	20	lo	hi
	JSR	RGCBP	;read char bit pattern	20	lo	hi
	JSR	LOGIC	;do required action and	20	lo	hi
	JSR	WBPGC	;write character back.	20	lo	hi
MPEND	JMP	LDTMP	;exit restoring regs.	4C	lo	hi

;CAPTI – Address screen location holding graphics character
;or byte containing pixel in TMPL-H. Adjust remainders to
;index Pixel Table, PXTAB, in Y.
;BG and PB version. YPIX for BG is 2, for PB is 3.
;Length – 43. Stack – 1.

RDIFF	EQU	nn	;vertical byte diff.	nn	
YPIX	EQU	yy	;*y* pixels per block.	yy	
CAPTI	LDA	GOH	;move origin hi-byte	A5	31
	STA	TMPH	;to TEMP store.	85	03
	LDA	PLTX	;divide *x* coordinate by	A5	34
	LSR	A	;2 giving byte offset,	4A	
	PHP		;saving remainder,	08	
	CLC		;added to origin with	18	
	ADC	GOL	;any carry into high	65	30
	STA	TMPL	;byte, giving correct	85	02
	BCC	CAPY	;column on bottom	90	02
	INC	TMPH	;line in TMPL-H.	E6	03
CAPY	LDY	PLTY	;get *y* pixels offset.	A4	35
CASL	TYA		;loop: remainder to A	98	
	SEC		;subtract pixels per	38	

```
            SBC    #YPIX          ;block, exit loop if      E9  yy
            BCC    CACI           ;no full block left,      90  0D
            TAY                   ;else remainder to Y.     A8
            LDA    TMPL           ;subtract row byte        A5  02
            SBC    #RDIFF         ;difference, moving        E9  nn
            STA    TMPL           ;address up one line      85  02
            BCS    CASL           ;until TMPL-H addresses   B0  F1
            DEC    TMPH           ;correct location.        C6  03
            BCC    CASL           ;                         90  ED
CACI        TYA                   ;use y remainder and      98
            PLP                   ;x remainder to form      28
            ROL    A              ;PXTAB index output       2A
            TAY                   ;in Y.                    A8
            RTS                   ;end CAPTI module.        60
;CAPTI – HR version. Length – 38. Stack – 0.
RDIFF       EQU    nn             ;vertical byte diff.       nn
CAPTI       LDA    GOH            ;move origin hi-byte      A5  31
            STA    TMPH           ;to TEMP store.           85  03
            LDA    PLTX           ;divide x coordinate by   A5  34
            LSR    A              ;8 giving byte offset     4A
            LSR    A              ;from origin,             4A
            LSR    A              ;added to                 4A
            CLC                   ;origin lo-byte with      18
            ADC    GOL            ;any carry in to hi-byte  65  30
            BCC    CAPY           ;giving correct column    90  02
            INC    TMPH           ;in A-TMPH.               E6  03
CAPY        LDY    PLTY           ;get y pixels offset.     A4  35
            BEQ    CALB           ;skip if bottom line.     F0  0A
CASL        SEC                   ;else loop: subtract      38
            SBC    #RDIFF         ;row byte difference       E9  nn
            BCS    CASLT          ;for each y dot           B0  02
            DEC    TMPH           ;displacement, moving     C6  03
CASLT       DEY                   ;address up one line      88
            BNE    CASL           ;until correct byte       D0  F6
CALB        STA    TMPL           ;addressed by TMPL-H.     85  02
            LDA    PLTX           ;x remainder forms        A5  34
            AND    #%00000111     ;PXTAB index output       29  07
            TAY                   ;in Y.                    A8
            RTS                   ;end CAPTI module.        60
```

;RGCBP – Read character from display memory, converting if
;necessary to LOGIC compatible sequential bit pattern in A.
;BG version. Requires 16-byte conversion table, BGTAB.
;Length – 16. Stack – 0.

```
RGCBP       LDX    #0             ;zero index address and   A2  00
            LDA    (TMPL,X)       ;pick up addressed byte.  A1  02
```

```
            LDX   #15          ;index BGTAB last byte.A2  0F
RGCL        CMP   BGTAB,X      ;compare with possible  DD  lo   hi
            BEQ   RGBP         ;patterns, ending if    F0  03
            DEX                ;match, else continue   CA
            BNE   RGCL         ;until blank pattern.    D0  F8
RGBP        TXA                ;place becomes pattern.  8A
            RTS                ;end RGCBP module.       60
BGTAB       EQB   $60,$7E,$7C  ;table of PET            60  7E   7C
            EQB   $78,$7B,$61  ;quarter square          78  7B   61
            EQB   $FF,$EC,$6C  ;graphics. See           FF  EC   6C
            EQB   $7F,$E1,$FB  ;Figure 12.1             7F  E1   FB
            EQB   $F8,$FC,$FE  ;                        F8  FC   FE
            EQB   $E0          ;                        E0
;RGCBP – PB and HR version. No table needed.
;Length – 5. Stack – 0.
RGCBP       LDX   #0           ;zero index address and  A2  00
            LDA   (TMPL,X)     ;pick up bit pattern.     A1  02
            RTS                ;end RGCBP module.        60
;LOGIC – Carry out action specified in PLTM on bit pattern
;in A using pixel bit table, PXTAB, indexed by Y. Set bit 0
;of PLTR if result set. Only PXTAB differs for different
;graphics types. Length – 29. Stack – 0.
LOGIC       LDX   PLTM         ;pick up mode.            A6  38
            BEQ   LPTST        ;0 = TEST only.           F0  0F
            EOR   PXTAB,Y      ;bit  NOT bit.            59  lo   hi
            DEX                ;skip if mode             CA
            BEQ   LPTST        ;was 1 = INVERT.          F0  09
            ORA   PXTAB,Y      ;bit  SET.                19  lo   hi
            DEX                ;skip if mode             CA
            BEQ   LPTST        ;was 2 = PLOT.            F0  03
            EOR   PXTAB,Y      ;bit  RESET (UNPLOT).59   lo   hi
LPTST       TAX                ;save result byte and     AA
            AND   PXTAB,Y      ;test bit. If result bit  39  lo   hi
            BEQ   LEND         ;reset then skip, else    F0  02
            INC   PLTR         ;set bit 0 of PLTR.       E6  39
LEND        TXA                ;result back to A.        8A
            RTS                ;end LOGIC module.        60

;PXTAB – BG version. Bits 0, 1, 2 and 3.
PXTAB       EQB   $04,$08      ;lower-left, lower-right  04  08
            EQB   $01,$02      ;upper-left, upper-right  01  02

;PXTAB – PB version. Bits 0, 1, 2, 3, 4 and 6.
PXTAB       EQB   $10,$40      ;lower-left, lower-right  10  40
            EQB   $04,$08      ;mid-left, mid-right      04  08
            EQB   $01,$02      ;upper-left, upper-right  01  02
```

```
;PXTAB – HR version. All bits.
PXTAB   EQB   $80,$40      ;leftmost dot to ...        80    40
        EQB   $20,$10      ;                           20    10
        EQB   $08,$04      ;                           08    04
        EQB   $02,$01      ;... right-most dot.        02    01
```

;WBPGC – Write character in A to display memory addressed
;by TMPL-H, converting if necessary from LOGIC compatible
;sequential bit pattern to graphics character.
;BG version. Uses BGTAB for conversion (see RGCBP).
;Length – 9. Stack 0.

```
WBPGC   TAX                ;bit pattern becomes        AA
        LDA   BGTAB,X      ;table index. Get byte,     BD   lo    hi
        LDX   #0           ;zero index address and     A2   00
        STA   (TMPL,X)     ;put byte to display.       81   02
        RTS                ;end WBPGC module.          60
```

;WBPGC – PB and HR version. No conversion needed.
;Length – 5. Stack – 0.

```
WBPGC   LDX   #0           ;zero index address and     A2   00
        STA   (TMPL,X)     ;put byte to display.       81   02
        RTS                ;end WBPGC module.          60
```

Chapter Thirteen
Lines and Shapes

The next stage after plotting a single point is to draw a straight line from A to B. The routine MDRAW assumes the coordinates at PLTX-Y to be those of a point already plotted and draws a line from there to, and including, the point with coordinates in DRWX-Y. Since MPLOT is called to plot each point, the entire line can be modally drawn.

The algorithm used in MDRAW may seem a little obscure but is necessary to obtain the correct steps between rows and columns. Figure 13.1 illustrates the need. Lines (a) and (c) are drawn between the same pair of points. The step spacing in (a) appears the more even of the two but when the line is extended, as in (b) and (d), it becomes clear that the second type of spacing – that used in MDRAW – is really the most even.

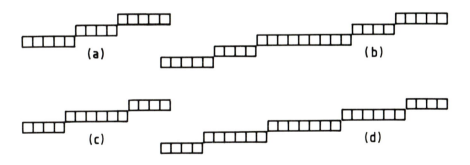

Fig. 13.1. Different steps.

MDRAW treats all coordinates as unsigned values in the range 0 to 255 with the origin at the bottom left of the display. This makes it incompatible with any routines which deal with signed coordinates in the range −128 to +127, as do the shape-changing routines in the next chapter. Figure 13.2 shows how areas referenced by unsigned and signed single-byte coordinates overlap.

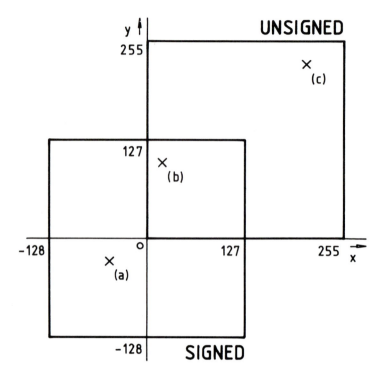

Fig. 13.2. Overlap of signed byte and unsigned byte areas.

It would be possible to write MPLOT and MDRAW to act on signed coordinates and have an origin near the centre of the display. However, the bottom left origin is generally more useful and a good deal easier to work with. Movement, or *translation*, of sets of coordinates is quite simple and can be used to achieve compatibility between the use of signed and unsigned numbers. A routine to do this is given in the next chapter.

The only real problem caused by the conflicting ranges is when a line crosses either of the two axes. In Figure 13.2, a line intended to run from (−50, −30) at point (a) to (10, 100) at point (b) will be drawn by MDRAW from (206, 226) at point (c) to point (b). The reason for this is that (c) is the unsigned equivalent of (a). As (b) is within the overlap area, it is the same in both signed and unsigned number systems.

MDRAW – Modal draw from PLTX-Y to DRWX-Y
Subroutines – PSHZM, PULZM, MUG, MPLOT.
Length – 96.
Stack – 7. User stack – 8.

Input – *x,y* (from) coordinates in PLTX, PLTY.

   x,y (to) coordinates in DRWX, DRWY.

   Plot mode (1 to 3) in PLTM.

Output – The line, or any part of it within the display area defined by the variables stored in $30 to $33, is modally drawn.

Registers changed – None.

Method – The absolute difference between coordinate-from and coordinate-to is found for y-values and then x-values, along with step values: +1 for low to high or −1 for high to low. Use the greater difference to determine the number of points to plot, ending if it is zero. The greater difference coordinate is stepped every iteration but the lesser difference coordinate is stepped only when a step counter falls below zero on subtraction of the lesser difference. The step counter is initialised to the greatest integer less than half of the greatest difference and on falling below zero, the greatest difference is added. The line is thus stepped evenly with half-length steps at each end.

				lo	hi
MDRAW	JSR	PSHZM	;save APYX, User A & B 20	lo	hi
	EQB	$04,$FF	;on user stack.	04	FF
	CLD		;for binary arithmetic.	D8	
	LDX	#1	;loop: index *y* then *x*:	A2	01
MDDL	LDY	#+1	;step low to high…	A0	01
	SEC		;get 'to' minus 'from'	38	
	LDA	DRWX,X	;difference and skip	B5	36
	SBC	PLTX,X	;out if positive else	F5	34
	BCS	MDSD	;Y becomes step value	B0	07
	LDY	#−1	;for high to low, get	A0	FF
	SEC		;absolute difference.	38	
	LDA	PLTX,X	;*x*-difference goes to	B5	34
	SBC	DRWX,X	;UAL, *y*-diff to UAH.	F5	36
MDSD	STA	UAL,X	;step value for PLTX to 95	08	
	STY	UBL,X	;UBL, for PLTY to UBH. 94	0A	
	DEX		;*y*-coords for X = 1,	CA	
	BPL	MDDL	;*x*-coords for X = 0.	10	E9
	JSR	MUG	;greater diff in UAH	20	lo hi
	EQB	$08,$05	;using sort in MUG.	08	05
	LDX	#1	;index *y* if *y*-diff >=	A2	01
	BCC	MDCG	;*x*-diff on SRT output,	90	01
	DEX		;else index *x*.	CA	
MDCG	LDY	UAH	;end if greatest diff is	A4	09
	BEQ	MDWND	;zero (no line) else A	F0	2D
	DEY		;is greatest integer <	88	
	TYA		;half greatest diff as	98	

	LSR	A	;step count. Y is the	4A		
	INY		;greatest diff counter.	C8		
MDPL	SEC		;loop: subtract lesser	38		
	SBC	UAL	;diff from step counter,	E5	08	
	BCS	MDMG	;skip if subtract okay	B0	15	
	ADC	UAH	;else below 0 so add	65	09	
	PHA		;greater diff to step	48		
	CLC		;counter and step both	18		
	LDA	PLTX	;coordinates, saving	A5	34	
	ADC	UBL	;step count on stack	65	0A	
	STA	PLTX	;during step.	85	34	
	CLC		;	18		
	LDA	PLTY	;	A5	35	
	ADC	UBH	;	65	0B	
	STA	PLTY	;	85	35	
	PLA		;restore step counter,	68		
	SEC		;ensure branch occurs,	38		
	BCS	MDCP	;and skip to plot.	B0	09	
MDMG	PHA		;save step counter and	48		
	CLC		;step only greater diff	18		
	LDA	PLTX,X	;coordinate, which is *x*	B5	34	
	ADC	UBL,X	;for X = 0 and *y* for	75	0A	
	STA	PLTX,X	;X = 1.	95	34	
	PLA		;restore step counter.	68		
MDCP	JSR	MPLOT	;modal plot point *x,y*.	20	lo	hi
	DEY		;repeat for all units	88		
	BNE	MDPL	;of greater difference.	D0	D7	
MDWND	JSR	PULZM	;restore user B & A and	20	lo	hi
	EQB	$04,$FF	;XYPA from user stack.	04	FF	
	RTS		;return.	60		

Shape tables

A series of lines, which may be used to draw outline or 'matchstick' figures, can be stored as a table of end-point coordinates. The array storage area addressed by ARRL-H can be used to store up to 256 of these tables, numbered $00 to $FF.

Two information bytes are needed at the start of each table – as in a normal two-dimensional array. The first of these must hold the value 4 or 5, this being the number of bytes describing each line. The second information byte is the number of lines in the table (1 to 255).

Each line is described by 4 or 5 sequential bytes. The first byte gives the *x*-from coordinate, the second gives the *y*-from coordinate.

The third and fourth bytes give the *x*-to and *y*-to coordinates. The fifth byte is the plot mode. This is optional but if included allows each line to be plotted, unplotted or inverted independently.

The routine SDRAW moves the parameters for each line in turn to the page zero graphics variables at $34 to $37 or $38 and calls MPLOT to plot the first point and MDRAW to draw the line. SDRAW needs the shape table address and information bytes to be in the user registers A and B. ARRAY (Chapter 3) is used to fetch this information from storage:

STINF	JSR	PSHZM	;save APYX, user A & B	20	lo	hi
	EQB	$04,$FF	;on user stack.	04	FF	
	LDA	#nn	;shape table no. to A,	A9	nn	
	JSR	ARRAY	;info. to user A & B.	20	lo	hi
	JSR	SDRAW	;draw full shape.	20	lo	hi
	JSR	PULZM	;restore user B & A and	20	lo	hi
	EQB	$04,$FF	;XYPA from user stack.	04	FF	

If you want, the information in user registers A and B can be adjusted before calling SDRAW so that only a desired sub-sequence of lines from the shape table is drawn.

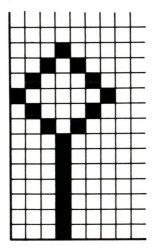

Fig. 13.3. Sample straight-line shape.

Figure 13.3 is the shape drawn using the values in the following table. It needs only a small display area of 7 pixels wide by 13 high. In the next chapter we will move this shape around the plane and perform various changes, or *transformations*, on it and a larger display area will be required. Before going on to that, however, you might like to draw the basic shape using different modes (the fifth byte in each line) and see what effect these have.

Information bytes:	$05	$06			
Line 1:	$03	$0C	$00	$09	$02
Line 2:	$03	$0C	$06	$09	$02
Line 3:	$03	$06	$00	$09	$02
Line 4:	$03	$06	$06	$09	$02
Line 5:	$03	$06	$03	$0C	$01
Line 6:	$03	$00	$03	$0C	$01

SDRAW – Shape table draw
Subroutines – PSHZM, PULZM, MPLOT, MDRAW.
Length – 43.
Stack – 9. *User stack –* 6.
Input – Address of byte preceding 1st line in UAL-H.
   Number of lines to draw in UBH.
   Number of bytes per line (4 or 5) in UBL. If UBL = 4 then plot mode in PLTM must be set for full table.
Output – All lines from shape table drawn.
Registers changed – None.
Method – For each line in the table: the parameters are copied into graphics information in page zero, MPLOT is called to plot the first point, then MDRAW to plot all other points to the line-end coordinates.

SDRAW	JSR	PSHZM	;save A,P,Y, UAL, UAH	20	lo	hi
	EQB	$04,$B7	;and UBH on user stack.	04	B7	
	CLD		;for binary addition.	D8		
SDLL	LDY	UBL	;index last byte of line	A4	0A	
SDBL	LDA	(UAL),Y	;loop: move parameters	B1	08	
	STA	PLTX-1,Y	;of current line to	99	33	00
	DEY		;correct graphics	88		
	BNE	SDBL	;variables.	D0	F8	
	JSR	MPLOT	;plot start point.	20	lo	hi
	JSR	MDRAW	;draw to end point.	20	lo	hi
	CLC		;address next line in	18		
	LDA	UAL	;table by adding no. of	A5	08	
	ADC	UBL	;bytes per line to	65	0A	
	STA	UAL	;address in user A.	85	08	
	BCC	SDLLT	;take care of any	90	02	
	INC	UAH	;carry to hi-byte.	E6	09	
SDLLT	DEC	UBH	;repeat for all lines	C6	0B	
	BNE	SDLL	;in shape table.	D0	E1	

```
JSR    PULZM      ;restore information to  20   lo   hi
EQB    $04,$B7    ;UBH, UAH-L& Y, P& A. 04   B7
RTS               ;return.                 60
```

Chapter Fourteen

Changing Shapes

In this last chapter on coordinate graphics we move shapes across the plane (one solution to the overlapping range problem of Chapter 13), reflect them, reduce them to half size, rotate them about the origin and make them lean to the side. All of these changes are accomplished by simple 8-bit addition or shifts.

Translation

Translation is the moving of a point by a given distance and in a given direction. It is carried out by adding one value to the x coordinate and another value to the y coordinate. This pair of values is known as a *vector* and the process as *vector addition*. Adding a positive value to the x coordinate will cause the point to move to the right; adding a negative value will move it to the left. The same applies to the y coordinate but the movement is in this case up or down.

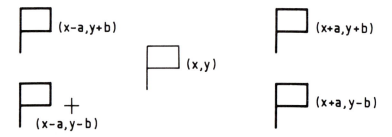

Fig. 14.1. Translation in four directions.

When the same vector is added to all of the coordinate-pairs in a shape table the entire shape is moved to a new position. Figure 14.1 shows translation of a small flag in four directions using positive and negative values of a vector (a, b). Translation can be used to move shapes from any part of the plane to that part covered by the display area. It can also be used to simulate movement of a shape across the screen by repeatedly unplotting, translating, plotting.

The routine PTLT translates a single point with coordinates in DRWX-Y by adding the vector in TLTX-Y. Since 8-bit addition is used, a movement off one side of the signed byte area of the plane (see Chapter 13) will move the point on to the opposite side. This is known as *wraparound* for quite obvious reasons. SCHNG, later in this chapter, will translate a complete shape table figure by calling PTLT to move individual points.

PTLT – Point translation
Subroutines – STTMP, LDTMP.
Length – 19.
Stack – 3.
Input – Point coordinates in DRWX-Y. Vector in TLTX-Y.
Output – Point coordinates changed.
Registers changed – None.
Method – 8-bit addition of vector value to coordinate.

PTLT	JSR	STTMP	;save regs in TEMP store.	20	lo	hi
	CLD		;for binary addition.	D8		
	LDX	#1	;index *y* first in loop.	A2	01	
PTTL	CLC		;add vector value to	18		
	LDA	DRWX,X	;coordinate, 8-bit	B5	36	
	ADC	TLTX,X	;wraparound addition.	75	3A	
	STA	DRWX,X	;new coordinate back.	95	36	
	DEX		;do it for	CA		
	BPL	PTTL	;both coordinates.	10	F6	
	JMP	LDTMP	;restore regs, return.	4C	lo	hi

Transformations

Many transformations of a shape may be carried out by forming new coordinates from the old by *matrix multiplication*. This is done by a cross-multiplication of 4 factors with the old coordinates as in Figure 14.2. The group of factors is known as the *transformation matrix*.

Multiplication, however, is slow, complex and unnecessary in many applications. By limiting the elements of the transformation matrix to +1, −1 or 0, multiplication reduces to simple addition or

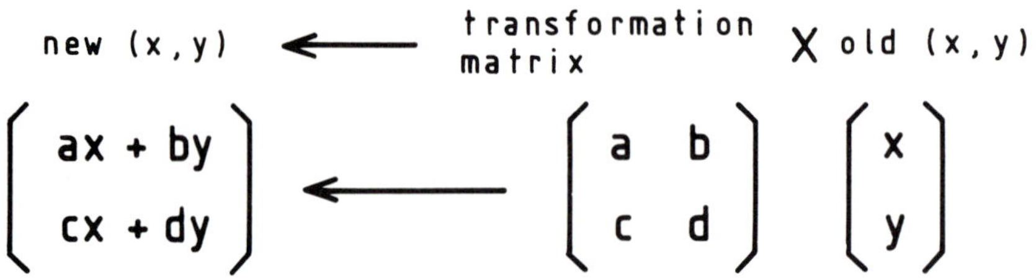

$$\text{new } (x,y) \quad \longleftarrow \quad \begin{matrix}\text{transformation}\\\text{matrix}\end{matrix} \quad X \text{ old } (x,y)$$

$$\begin{pmatrix} ax + by \\ cx + dy \end{pmatrix} \quad \longleftarrow \quad \begin{pmatrix} a & b \\ c & d \end{pmatrix} \begin{pmatrix} x \\ y \end{pmatrix}$$

Fig. 14.2. Matrix multiplication.

subtraction of the old coordinates and new x and y values can be formed from different combinations of 0, $+x$, $-x$, $+y$ and $-y$.

A single byte transformation code can be used to convey all necessary information with each pair of bits having the following meaning:

00    $+$old coordinate
01   no effect
10    $+$ old c. $-$ old c. (i.e. no effect)
11    $-$ old coordinate

Each new coordinate is formed from the old coordinate-pair by the actions caused by one hexadecimal digit of the code byte. The high order digit is responsible for the new x and the low order digit for the new y. Of the sixteen hexadecimal digits, only eight are of real use:

digit	action
0	$+x$ $+y$
1	$+x$
3	$+x$ $-y$
4	$+y$
7	$-y$
C	$-x$ $+y$
D	$-x$
F	$-x$ $-y$

Some transformation codes will cause all points to fall to one of four straight lines, to the origin or have no effect. Fifteen codes produce useful transformations and these are shown in Figs. 14.3 to 14.6.

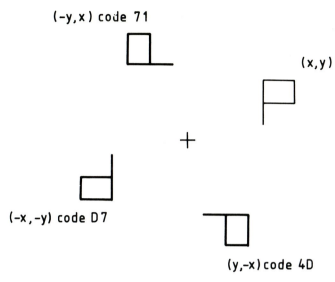

Fig. 14.3. 90°, 180° and 270° rotations.

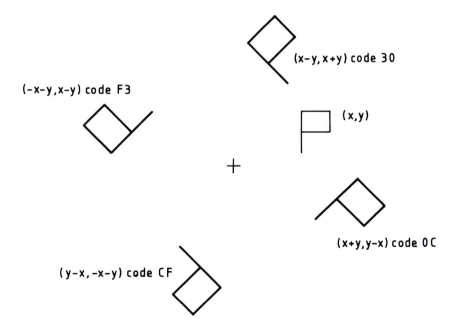

Fig. 14.4. 45°, 135°, 225° and 315° enlarging rotations.

PTFM, like PTLT, deals only with a single pair of coordinates in DRWX-Y. The transformation code in TFMC is rotated to access each bit in turn and the old coordinate values added or subtracted as

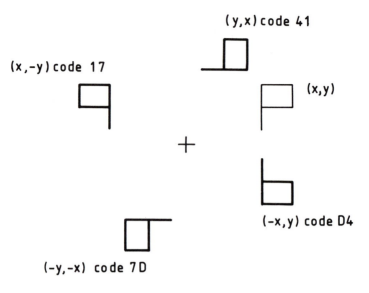

Fig. 14.5. Reflections in x=0, y=0, y=x and y=−x.

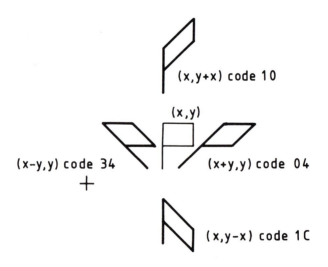

Fig. 14.6. x+, x−, y+ and y− shears.

appropriate. SCHNG will transform a full shape by calling PTFM to change individual points.

PTFM – Point transformation
Subroutines – STTMP, LDTMP.
Length – 42.
Stack – 3.

Input – Point coordinates in DRWX-Y.
  Transformation code in TFMC.
Output – Point coordinates change.
Registers changed – None.
Method – The transformation code is rotated bringing each bit out
  into carry in turn. Old coordinate values are added, subtracted or
  not to the initially zeroised new coordinate depending on the
  transformation code bits. New coordinates are saved on stack
  during this operation so as not to affect the values being added or
  subtracted.

PTFM	JSR	STTMP	;save regs in TEMP store.	20	lo	hi
	CLD		;for binary arithmetic.	D8		
	LDY	#2	;new coord. counter.	A0	02	
PTNCL	LDX	#1	;loop: index old *y* first	A2	01	
	LDA	#0	;clear new coordinate.	A9	00	
PTOCL	ROR	TFMC	;loop: shift add bit	66	3C	
	BCS	PTMA	;out, skip if no add	B0	03	
	ADC	DRWX,X	;else add old coord. &	75	36	
	CLC		;restore bit status	18		
PTMA	ROR	TFMC	;shift sub bit out	66	3C	
	BCC	PTMS	;skip if no sub	90	03	
	SBC	DRWX,X	;else sub old coord. &	F5	36	
	SEC		;restore bit status	38		
PTMS	DEX		;repeat for both old	CA		
	BPL	PTOCL	;coordinates, then put	10	EF	
	PHA		;new coord. on stack.	48		
	DEY		;repeat for two new	88		
	BNE	PTNCL	;coordinates on stack.	D0	E7	
	ROR	TFMC	;restore TFMC last bit.	66	3C	
	PLA		;move new *x* and *y*	68		
	STA	DRWX	;coordinates	85	36	
	PLA		;from stack	68		
	STA	DRWY	;to DRWX-Y.	85	37	
	JMP	LDTMP	;restore regs, return.	4C	lo	hi

Half linear reduction

The enlarging rotations (see Figure 14.4) magnify the distance of any
point from the origin by $\sqrt{2}$. This is unavoidable when using unit
values to produce the transformations. It is useful in that a shape may
be doubled in size by two successive transformations of this type.
  There is no transformation, or combination of transformations,

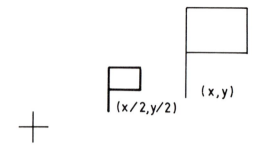

Fig. 14.7. Half linear reduction.

using unit values which will effect a corresponding reduction in size. This requires a special routine. PHLF halves the distance between a single point with coordinates in DRWX-Y and the origin. It will be called by SCHNG to halve all dimensions of a complete shape. Figure 14.7 shows the effect of half linear reduction on our little flag.

In unsigned arithmetic, a simple logical shift right (LSR) will divide a binary number by two, chopping off any fraction. Signed arithmetic is more difficult since negative values must have a 1 shifted into the sign bit (arithmetic shift right) and, to achieve symmetry with positive numbers, must be rounded up towards zero – hence the increment and setting of Carry in that part of PHLF dealing dealing with negative coordinates.

PHLF – Halve distance from point to origin
Subroutines – STTMP, LDTMP.
Length – 21.
Stack – 3.
Input – Point coordinates in DRWX-Y.
Output – Coordinates halved and rounded towards zero.
Registers changed – None.
Method – Carry is set or reset to copy the coordinate sign bit so that a rotate right acts as an arithmetic right shift. Negative values are also incremented before the shift to ensure rounding towards zero.

PHLF	JSR	STTMP	;save regs in TEMP store.	20	lo	hi
	LDX	#1	;index *y* coord. first.	A2	01	
PHFL	CLC		;loop: positive new sign	18		
	LDY	DRWX,X	;test current sign bit	B4	36	
	BPL	PHFH	;and skip if positive	10	03	
	INC	DRWX,X	;else round fraction up	F6	36	
	SEC		;negative new sign	38		

PHFH	ROR	DRWX,X	;arithmetic shift right.	76	36	
	DEX		;repeat for both *y* and	CA		
	BPL	PHFL	;*x* coordinates.	10	F3	
	JMP	LDTMP	;restore regs, return.	4C	lo	hi

Shape change

The three routines PTLT, PTFM and PHLF act only on the coordinates of a single point held in DRWX-Y. SCHNG acts on a complete shape held in a shape table by transferring each coordinate-pair to DRWX-Y and then calling the correct routine. An 'action code' has to be input to SCHNG for it to select the appropriate routine. The action code, in A, also tells SCHNG whether the registers X and Y hold a translation vector or transformation code. If they do, SCHNG stores these values in the correct graphics variables in page zero.

SCHNG is like SDRAW in that the shape table address must be in UAL-H, the number of bytes per line in UBL and the number of lines in UBH. The piece of code, STINF, given in Chapter 13 to initialise these variables for SDRAW can be used for SCHNG by changing JSR SDRAW to JSR SCHNG and by loading A with the action code and X and Y with the appropriate arguments before JSR SCHNG.

Since UAL-H and UBL-H are not changed by either SDRAW or SCHNG, the initialisation process in STINF needs only to be done once for a sequence of operations on any one shape table.

SCHNG – Shape table shape change
Subroutines – PSHZM, PULZM, PTLT, PTFM, PHLF.
Length – 83.
Stack – 7. *User stack* – 7.
Input – Address of byte preceding first line in UAL-H.
   Bytes per line (4 or 5) in UBL. No. of lines in UBH.
   Action code in A: =0: translation (vector in X, Y)
                     =1: transformation (code in X)
                     >1: halving (no arguments)
Output – Shape translated, transformed or halved.
Registers changed – None.
Method – The action code is tested and any input arguments stored appropriately. Each pair of coordinates is moved in turn to DRWX-Y, the action code tested and the appropriate subroutine called.

SCHNG	JSR	PSHZM	;save APYX, UAL-H and	20	lo	hi
	EQB	$04,$BF	;UBH on user stack.	04	BF	
	CLD		;for binary addition.	D8		
	CMP	#1	;test action code	C9	01	
	BCS	SCTF	;skip if not translate	B0	04	
	STX	TLTX	;else put vector	86	3A	
	STY	TLTY	;in TLTX-Y.	84	3B	
SCTF	BNE	SCPI	;skip if not transform	D0	02	
	STX	TFMC	;else code to TFMC.	86	3C	
SCPI	TAX		;action code to X.	AA		
SCLL	LDY	#4	;loop: index *y*-to byte	A0	04	
SCPL	LDA	(UAL),Y	;loop: move pair of	B1	08	
	STA	DRWY	;coordinates to	85	37	
	DEY		;DRWX-Y for routines	88		
	LDA	(UAL),Y	;dealing with	B1	08	
	STA	DRWX	;individual points.	85	36	
	INY		;index *y* again.	C8		
	CPX	#1	;test action code	E0	01	
	BCS	SCNTT	;skip if code >0	B0	05	
	JSR	PTLT	;else translate point	20	lo	hi
	BCC	SCCB	;and put back.	90	0A	
SCNTT	BNE	SCHF	;skip if code >1	D0	05	
	JSR	PTFM	;else transform point	20	lo	hi
	BEQ	SCCB	;and put back.	F0	03	
SCHF	JSR	PHLF	;code >1 so halve point	20	lo	hi
SCCB	LDA	DRWY	;move new coordinates	A5	37	
	STA	(UAL),Y	;from DRWX-Y	91	08	
	DEY		;back to replace old	88		
	LDA	DRWX	;coordinates	A5	36	
	STA	(UAL),Y	;in table.	91	08	
	DEY		;do for both points	88		
	BNE	SCPL	;in each line.	D0	D7	
	CLC		;address next line in	18		
	LDA	UAL	;table by adding no. of	A5	08	
	ADC	UBL	;bytes per line to	65	0A	
	STA	UAL	;address in UAL-H	85	08	
	BCC	SCLLT	;add any carry	90	02	
	INC	UAH	;to hi-byte.	E6	09	
SCLLT	DEC	UBH	;repeat for all	C6	0B	
	BNE	SCLL	;lines in table.	D0	C6	
	JSR	PULZM	;restore UBH, UAH-L &	20	lo	hi
	EQB	$04,$BF	;XYPA from user stack.	04	BF	
	RTS		;return.	60		

Patterns and symmetry

The most striking point about many of the transformations is their symmetrical nature. A less immediately obvious fact is that a single transformation is often the equivalent of two or more different transformations and an original shape can be recovered very easily even after the most extensive sequence of such changes.

The program subroutine PATTN uses the shape table given in Chapter 13, centring the shape above the origin to perform the transformations and then translating it to be drawn centred on a display area 40 pixels high by 64 wide. On a smaller format screen the top and right of the pattern could be lost. A representation of the complete pattern is shown in Fig. 14.8.

Fig. 14.8. Displayed pattern.

The program which calls PATTN must have cleared the display to graphics spaces, initialised the page zero variables and loaded A with the array number where the shape table is stored.

PATTN	JSR	PSHZM	;save APYX, user A & B	20	lo	hi
	EQB	$04,$FF	;on user stack.	04	FF	
	JSR	ARRAY	;get shape table info.	20	lo	hi
	LDA	#0	;translate shape to	A9	00	
	LDX	#−3	;be centred	A2	FD	
	LDY	#+3	;above origin.	A0	03	
	JSR	SCHNG	;	20	lo	hi
	LDA	#1	;transformation code.	A9	01	
	LDX	#$0C	;rotate 315° twice	A2	0C	
	JSR	SCHNG	;to double size and	20	lo	hi

JSR	TDTD	;translated draw it.	20	lo	hi
LDX	#$41	;reflect in $y = x$	A2	41	
JSR	SCHNG	;	20	lo	hi
LDX	#$7D	;reflect in $y = -x$	A2	7D	
JSR	TDTD	;and draw.	20	lo	hi
LDA	#2	;reduce to start size	A9	02	
JSR	SCHNG	;by halving.	20	lo	hi
LDA	#1	;transform code again	A9	01	
LDX	#$71	;rotate 90°	A2	71	
JSR	TDTD	;and draw.	20	lo	hi
LDX	#$34	;shear x decreases and	A2	34	
JSR	DRCR	;draw reflection series.	20	lo	hi
LDX	#$04	;shear x increases and	A2	04	
JSR	DRCR	;draw reflection series.	20	lo	hi
LDX	#$04	;shear x increases twice	A2	04	
JSR	SCHNG	;to recover original	20	lo	hi
JSR	SCHNG	;shape, then rotate	20	lo	hi
LDX	#$D7	;180° to original	A2	D7	
JSR	TDTD	;position and draw.	20	lo	hi
LDA	#0	;restore shape to	A9	00	
LDX	#+3	;position on entry to	A2	03	
LDY	#−3	;PATTN before exit.	A0	FD	
JSR	SCHNG	;	20	lo	hi
JSR	PULZM	;restore UBH-L, UAH-L	20	lo	hi
EQB	$04,$FF	;and XYPA from user	04	FF	
RTS		;stack and return.	60		

;draw series of reflections about two axes.

DRCR	JSR	TDTD	;draw at current	20	lo	hi
	LDX	#$D4	;position, then after	A2	D4	
	JSR	TDTD	;reflection in $y = 0$,	20	lo	hi
	LDX	#$17	;then after	A2	17	
	JSR	TDTD	;reflection in $x = 0$,	20	lo	hi
	LDX	#$D4	;then after reflection	A2	D4	
	JSR	TDTD	;in $y = 0$ again.	20	lo	hi
	RTS		;return to PATTN.	60		

;transform, translate, draw, translate and delay.

TDTD	JSR	SCHNG	;current transform then	20	lo	hi
	LDA	#0	;translation code for	A9	00	
	LDX	#+31	;centring pattern at	A2	1F	
	LDY	#+19	;(31, 19) for screen	A0	13	
	JSR	SCHNG	;fit.	20	lo	hi
	JSR	SDRAW	;draw shape in positive	20	lo	hi
	LDX	#−31	;coord. area, then	A2	E1	
	LDY	#−19	;translate back for	A0	ED	
	JSR	SCHNG	;further transforms.	20	lo	hi

```
LDA    #1           ;restore transform code.  A9  01
JSR    DL1S         ;delay 1 second.          20  lo    hi
RTS                 ;return to DRCR/PATTN. 60
```

Chapter Fifteen
Communicating

All personal computers have some means of communicating between the processor and external devices, such as keyboards, television sets, cassette recorders, printers and disk drives. Just what is provided varies widely between different equipment and, even where the same facilities are provided, the manner of implementing them depends on design detail that differs greatly from one machine to another.

In this chapter, we describe some of the general facilities available for communicating with the 6502 processor, as a basis from which you can start to look at what you have in your own equipment.

Input and output between external devices is channelled through ports. Processor manufacturers also make integrated circuits for controlling data through ports and it is quite common for a port controller of one manufacturer to be working in a system with another manufacturer's processor.

Input/output devices can often be configured by software, having a number of registers, the setting of which determines how the device operates, as well as registers to hold the data to be received or transmitted. In some systems these separate registers are assigned different port numbers by which they can be addressed. In others they are assigned memory addresses and can be written to or read from like any other RAM locations. Since the 6502 has no instructions for input and output from and to port numbers, any input/output devices used with it must be memory-mapped. To make the most of your computer, you will want to know what input/output devices it has and what memory locations have been assigned to the control and data registers.

Imagine a situation where serial data is being read through a single wire from a cassette recorder. It comes via a port interface which converts the single bits into an 8-bit byte, for transfer in parallel along the data bus to the processor. The same device would also probably take parallel data from the processor and transmit it serially. If data is received at address $FEFF and status information at address $FEFE and bit 7 of the status register is set when a byte has been collected ready for input, this simple code will read a character from the cassette:

```
CSIN:   LDA   $FEFE     ;get port status.      AD  FE  FE
        BPL   CSIN      ;repeat if no input.   10  FB
        LDA   $FEFF     ;now get data and      AD  FF  FE
        RTS             ;return.               60
```

Typically, a serial/parallel interface will provide other information which could be checked, such as the correct receipt of the character start bit, a parity check and an overflow warning if an incoming character overwrites the previous one before it has been processed.

In this type of application, the processor is occupied the whole time the character is being received, repeatedly testing the device status register. Tying up the processor like this can be avoided by using the interrupt facilities, if they have been left available to you in your particular computer.

Interrupts

The 6502 processor has a reset line, which is treated as a special kind of interrupt, and two other control lines into it, which allow peripherals to interrupt it, by taking the lines to the low voltage, or binary zero, state.

The non-maskable interrupt (NMI) line to pin 6 of the processor has the highest priority and is always acted upon on completion of the current instruction, irrespective of the state of the interrupt disable flag in the processor status register. The interrupt request (IRQ) line to pin 4 will only cause an interrupt on going low, when the interrupt disable flag is off (0).

To work with the restart and interrupt lines, there are three vectors, through which the microprocessor can take the location in memory from which to fetch the next instruction. The NMI vector is fixed at locations $FFFA-B, the restart vector at $FFFC-D and the IRQ vector at $FFFE-F. In these vectors are the addresses (lo hi) which go into the program counter for the next instruction to be fetched.

At reset, the processor automatically sets the interrupt disable flag and gets the address from the vector at $FFFC-D into the program counter. There will have to be some code at this address in ROM to initialise the system and one of the first things it will have to do is to put a value in the stack pointer, so that any interrupt, which will use the stack, can be handled. The instructions LDX #$FF,TXS set the initial top of stack address to the usual $01FF. Input/output devices might be initialised, interrupts will usually be enabled by a CLI instruction, and control will be passed to the system's entry program, which could be a monitor or operating system or a language processor like BASIC, to await the user's first command. Full details of what your computer does on start up are in the code at the address given in $FFFC-D.

At a non-maskable interrupt, the current instruction is completed, the program counter and P register are placed on the stack, the address in the vector at $FFFA-B is put into the program counter and the interrupt disable flag is set. Code to service the interrupt is now executed until an RTI (return from interrupt) instruction restores the P register and program counter to its pre-interrupt state and normal processing is resumed. On home computers, the NMI service routine is usually all in ROM and reserved for the use of the computer maker. It must save and return unaltered any registers it uses other than P.

The IRQ interrupt operates in the same way as the NMI except that it is ignored unless the interrupt disable flag is reset (0) and the code to service the interrupt is at the address given at $FFFE-F. Since the P register containing the interrupt disable flag is saved when an IRQ interrupt is actioned and restored by the RTI instruction, interrupts are automatically enabled again for the resumption of normal processing. It is probable that the system software of your computer will use the IRQ and service it by some code in ROM. It could well provide for a jump to an address in RAM to service any interrupts other than its own, so that you can also use the IRQ. All is revealed in the code at the address given in $FFFE-F or perhaps even in the computer manual or user guide.

A software IRQ interrupt can be caused by the BRK instruction in a program. In this case, the return address placed on the stack is that of the BRK instruction +2. The interrupt service routine distinguishes a software break from a peripheral interrupt by the setting of the B flag in bit 4 of the P register, which is the last byte to have been placed on the stack. The BRK instruction is sometimes used by systems software but is sometimes available for program debugging.

The 6522 VIA

The aptly named Versatile Interface Adapter is one of the devices available for controlling data through ports. Made by the makers of the 6502 processor, it is often found in 6502, as well as other, systems. It is connected on one side to the processor data bus and control lines and on the other side, for control of peripherals, has:

(1) 2 fully programmable 8-bit bi-directional input/output ports, known as Port A and Port B.
(2) One serial-to-parallel/parallel-to-serial shift register.
(3) Two 16-bit programmable counter/timers.
(4) Handshaking capability by which a computer and peripheral device can inform one another when they are ready to transmit or receive data.

The VIA is programmed through 16 registers which are accessed through the RAM memory addresses assigned to them in a particular system:

XXX0 Port B input/output register. Input when read; output when written to.
XXX1 Port A input/output register.
XXX2 Port B data direction register. 0 = input; 1 = output.
XXX3 Port A data direction register.
XXX4 Timer 1 latch/counter lo. Latch on a write.
XXX5 Timer 1 latch/counter hi. Counter on a read.
XXX6 Timer 1 latch lo.
XXX7 Timer 1 latch hi.
XXX8 Timer 2 latch/counter lo.
XXX9 Timer 2 counter hi.
XXXA Shift register.
XXXB Auxiliary control. For timer and shift registers.
XXXC Peripheral control. For handshaking data in and out.
XXXD Interrupt flag register.
XXXE Interrupt enable register.
XXXF Port A I/O register. As XXX1 but without handshaking.

Full details of how these registers are used to program the device are given in the manufacturer's data sheet. We will just look here at setting the VIA to transmit bytes, from an interrupt service routine, in parallel through Port B at XXX0.
So that all the data lines at Port B act as outputs, the data

direction register at XXX2 will need to be set to all ones. LDA #$FF, STA XXX2 will do this.

As well as the 8 data lines, there will be 2 control lines, CB2 and CB1, physically connecting the VIA and the peripheral. CB2 will give the 'data ready' signal, when a byte is stored in XXX0. CB1 will receive the 'data taken' signal back from the peripheral, and this signal will set the internal CB1 interrupt flag (bit 4) in XXXD and clear the 'data ready' output. For this transmission handshaking, bits 7,6 and 5 of the peripheral control register at XXXC must be set to 100 and, to set the interrupt flag, bit 4 of the peripheral control register must be 0. Bits 3 to 0 of the peripheral control register are used to control Port A. LDA #$80, ORA XXXC, STA XXXC would set Port B peripheral control without affecting Port A.

The IRQ line to the processor is actioned (goes low) and bit 7 in XXXD is set whenever an interrupt flag is set in XXXD and the corresponding bit in the interrupt enable register at XXXE is also set. Therefore, bit 4 of the interrupt enable register must be set if the CB1 line is to interrupt the processor. Setting selected bits in the interrupt enable register is done by writing to it with bit 7 in the byte set to 1. Then each 1 in bits 6 to 0 of the byte will set the corresponding bit in the interrupt enable register, whilst each 0 will leave it unaffected. LDA #$90, STA XXXE will set bit 4 of the interrupt enable register. To clear selected bits of the interrupt enable register, bit 7 of the byte written to it is 0. Then each 1 in bits 6 to 0 of the byte will clear the corresponding bit in the interrupt enable register and each 0 will leave it unaffected.

When interrupts from the VIA have been accepted for servicing, bit 7 of the interrupt flag register needs to be cleared. Interrupt flags are cleared by writing a 1 directly into the appropriate bit of the interrupt flag register at XXXD. LDA XXXD, STA XXXD will therefore get the state of the interrupt flags in A and clear bit 7 and any interrupt flags which were set.

Chapter Sixteen
Wrinkles

Wrinkles are the short effective methods used to perform commonly occurring tasks. The way to do these tasks neatly and efficiently is not always so obvious to the newcomer to machine code who might use up dozens of program bytes when the process can be done with a mere half dozen or so.

It is always worth scanning published listings for better ways of writing these essential processes. You will find quite a few of them in this book written as *utility* subroutines and several more written into the larger routines.

This chapter contains a collection of some of the more important wrinkles that you are likely to need. They act on the accumulator, the carry flag and on a 16-bit value in page zero memory. As always in 6502 machine code, the low order byte (VLB) precedes the high order byte (VHB).

16-bit counters

Using 8-bit counters is quite easy. The 6502 instruction set has specific instructions to increment or decrement the index registers or a memory byte. These instructions set the zero flag if the result is zero or reset it if the result is not zero. Using 16-bit counters is not so simple.

Incrementing a 16-bit value is the most straightforward. The hi-byte has to be incremented only if the lo-byte reaches 0 (i.e. 255 + 1 = 256 = $00).

```
        INC    VLB         ;add 1 to lo-byte.       E6   pq
        BNE    NEXT        ;only if lo-byte = 0     D0   02
        INC    VHB         ;is hi-byte inc'd.       E6   pr
NEXT    (next instruction)
```

When decrementing a 16-bit value, the hi-byte has to be decremented along with the lo-byte if the lo-byte is 0 before the decrement. So a test for zero has to be made at the start.

```
        LDA   VLB      ;test if lo-byte = 0      A5  pq
        BNE   DECLO    ;only if zero does        D0  02
        DEC   VHB      ;hi-byte get dec'd.       C6  pr
DECLO   DEC   VLB      ;take 1 from lo-byte.     C6  pq
```

After the 16-bit increment the zero flag will give the correct result but not so after the decrement. If the result is needed for a loop test, then a check will have to be made on both hi- and lo-bytes to see if they are zero.

```
        LDA   VLB      ;pick up lo-byte and       A5  pq
        ORA   VHB      ;hi-byte bits, looping     05  pr
        BNE   LOOP     ;only if not all reset.    D0  xx
```

Complementing the carry flag

The carry flag is often used to convey information between different parts of a program as well as its normal uses in arithmetic and logical operations. Sometimes we need it to be the opposite of what it is when we get it. The following sequence will complement C and set N and Z according to the value in A. A is not affected.

```
        ROL   A            ;move C to bit 0, A.      2A
        EOR   #%00000001   ;complement it.           49   01
        ROR   A            ;move complement back.    6A
```

Software switching

Some computer functions, such as sound, are achieved by sending out set and reset bits alternately to an output port. The switch from set to reset, and vice versa, can be done quite simply by exclusive-oring the accumulator with the same value as in the following loop.

```
        LDA   #0            ;clear bit initially.      A9  00
        LDX   #COUNT        ;number of pulses.         A2  xx
LOOP    STA   OUTP          ;send bit out.             8D  pq  rs
        JSR   DELAY         ;get right frequency.      20  lo  hi
        EOR   #%01000000    ;set/reset bit 6,A.        49  40
        DEX                 ;loop until number of      CA
        BNE   LOOP          ;pulses done.              D0  F5
```

Indexing the stack

We can get to any byte stored on the stack quite simply by transferring the value in the stack pointer to the X register and then using an absolute indexed instruction. For example, to pick up the value stored at a depth of 4 bytes on the stack we would write:

```
TSX                 ;index stack with X.      BA
LDA    $0104,X      ;get 4th deep byte.       BD   04   01
```

The byte currently at the top of the stack would be indexed by $0101,X.

Subraction by complement addition

Subtracting a value stored in memory from that in the accumulator is simple. You have to be a little more devious if you want to subtract the value in the accumulator from one stored in memory:

```
EOR    #$FF         ;complement subtrahend.   49   FF
SEC                 ;set as for SBC           38
ADC    MEMORY       ;add to complement.       65   pq
```

Complement addition is the process used by the 6502 for subtraction so this sequence mimics the SBC instruction. The carry flag result is as if a SBC instruction had been done.

Hexadecimal digit to ASCII code

Hexadecimal (base 16) numbers confusingly use the letters A to F to stand for the values 10 to 15. One major problem is the conversion between hex digits stored in 4 bits and the ASCII codes since there is a gap between ASCII 9 ($39) and ASCII A ($41). Conversion from ASCII to hex has to treat the two groups separately but, with the aid of decimal mode, arithmetic conversion from hex to ASCII is quick and easy.

Starting with the hex digit in the lowest 4 bits of the accumulator, and with the highest 4 bits cleared, the decimal addition of 90 to digits 0 to 9 results in values 90 to 99 with C reset. Addition of 40 then results in values 30 to 39 with C set. These last values are the hex-pair ASCII codes for 0 to 9. Adding 90 to digits A to F results in values 0 to 5 with C set. Addition with carry of 40 then results in values 41 to 46 which are the hex-pair ASCII codes for A to F.

```
SED                  ;for decimal addition      F8
CLC                  ;add without carry         18
ADC    #$90          ;90 as a decimal number    69   90
ADC    #$40          ;then 40 as decimal.       69   40
CLD                  ;back to binary mode.      D8
```

Lower-case to upper-case

The only difference between the ASCII codes for upper-case letters and those for lower-case letters is that the lower-case codes have bit 5 set (1) and the upper-case codes have bit 5 reset (0). If you AND the code with $DF then bit 5 will be reset no matter what it was to begin with and all the codes will then be upper-case. This will save you having to press the shift key when you input letters.

Quick arithmetic

Multiplication and division by powers of 2 can be performed very quickly by using shift and rotate instructions. This is the equivalent to multiplying decimal numbers by ten by putting a zero on the end.
  The following routine multiplies a 16-bit value by 4:

```
ASL    VLB          ;lo-byte × 2, carry to      06   pq
ROL    VHB          ;hi-byte × 2                26   pr
ASL    VLB          ;lo-byte × 4, carry to      06   pq
ROL    VHB          ;hi-byte × 4.               26   pr
```

The next routine divides a 16-bit value by 2 and rounds the result:

```
LSR    VHB          ;hi-byte/2, carry to        46   pr
ROR    VLB          ;lo-byte/2. If carry        66   pq
BCC    END          ;reset then complete        90   06
INC    VLB          ;else round up result       E6   pq
BNE    END          ;by a 16-bit                D0   02
INC    VHB          ;increment.                 E6   pr
END:
```

Appendix A
The 6502 Instruction Set

The instruction set of the 6502 has only 56 different mnemonics (instruction names). Many of these instructions can act on memory that is addressed by different methods and so the total number of different instructions available to the 6502 programmer is, in fact, 151. These are set out in tables at the end of this appendix and are grouped by instruction type.

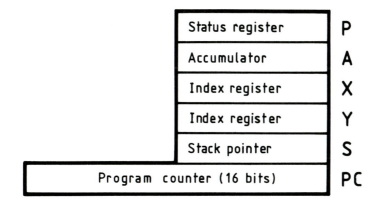

Status register	P
Accumulator	A
Index register	X
Index register	Y
Stack pointer	S
Program counter (16 bits)	PC

*Fig. A.1.*6502 register set.

For quick reference, brief notes on the 6502 registers (Fig. A.1), flags (Fig. A.2) and addressing modes are also given in this appendix. Except for the information which is specific to the computer system you are using – RAM addresses, system clock speed, video memory, etc. – this appendix contains all the information you will need when writing programs in 6502 machine code.

Registers

A	*Accumulator.* 8-bit register used mainly for arithmetic.
P	*Status register.* Not really an 8-bit register but a collection of 8 individual bits each with a different purpose. See *Flags.*
X and **Y**	*Index registers.* Two 8-bit registers used for several purposes: (a) as counters, (b) to index memory as an extension from a base address (see *addressing modes*), (c) for temporary storage of data.
S	*Stack pointer.* Points to an area of memory used mainly for storing program addresses during subroutine calls. The 6502 stack is fixed in page 1 of memory (at $0100 to $01FF). *S* supplies the lo-byte of the address. $0100+S is the address immediately below the last byte pushed.
PC	*Program counter.* The only 16-bit register of the 6502. It is inaccessible to the programmer except by *JMP* and *JSR* instructions which put new values into the *PC*. It is used by the processor as a pointer to the next instruction byte to be fetched from the program. You should always assume that, during the operation of an instruction, the *PC* points to the first byte of the next instruction.

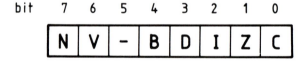

Fig. A.2. Status register P (flags).

Flags

N (P$_7$)	*Negative flag.* A copy of the sign bit of the result of an operation. In 2's complement signed numbers, $00 to $7F is positive (0 to 127 decimal) and $80 to $FF is negative (−128 to −1 decimal). Sometimes called *sign flag (S).*
V (P$_6$)	*Overflow flag.* Shows if arithmetic overflow has occurred. It is the result of exclusive-oring the carry-in

to the sign bit with the carry-out of the sign bit of the arithmetic result.

(P_5 is not used. You may find it always set, always reset or changing state for no known reason. Forget it!)

B (P_4)   *Break flag.* Set after a *BRK* (software interrupt) instruction to distinguish from an external interrupt.

D (P_3)   *Decimal mode flag.* If set, the 6502 will do binary coded decimal (BCD) arithmetic instead of binary. In BCD, each byte is used for two decimal digits from 0000 (0) to 1001 (9) and 1010 to 1111 codes are not used.

I (P_2)   *Interrupt disable flag.* External logic is allowed to interrupt the program and use the processor only if this flag is reset to 0.

Z (P_1)   *Zero flag.* Set if the result of an operation is zero (all bits reset). Don't trust it in Decimal mode arithmetic.

C (P_0)   *Carry flag.* Used to store a bit carried out of a result byte when 8 bits just are not enough. In subtraction, it is reset for a borrow and set if there is no borrow. *C* also takes the bit shifted out in a rotate or shift instruction.

Addressing modes

*Immediate data mode.* Tells the processor to use the data written as the second byte of the instruction. The hash symbol (#) is used by assemblers to distinguish data from addresses. For example, LDY #−1 (code A0 FF) puts the value $FF (decimal 255 or −1) into the Y register.

z   *Zero page direct.* The second instruction byte supplies the low order byte of an address in page zero (page zero is from $0000 to $00FF). For example, ROL $15 (code 26 15) does a left rotation of the byte stored at $0015.

ab   *Absolute direct.* The second and third instruction bytes give an absolute address anywhere from $0000 to $FFFF. The low order byte of the address is always written before the high order byte in the machine code. For example, ADC $AB12 (code 6D 12 AB) adds the value held in memory at location $AB12 to the accumulator – also adding the carry flag – and stores the result in the accumulator.

(ab)   *Indirect.* JMP is the only instruction to use this mode. For example, JMP (567) (code 6C 37 02) results in the byte stored at $0237 (decimal 567) being put into PC$_{lo}$ and that at $0238 (decimal 568) into PC$_{hi}$.

ab,X and   *Absolute indexed.* The value in X or Y is added to the
ab,Y   address given as second and third bytes and the result used as a pointer to data held in memory. For example, INC $00D6,X (code FE D6 00). If X = $A3 then the data byte held in $0179 (=$00D6 + $00A3) will have 1 added to it.

z,X and   *Zero page indexed.* The value in X or Y is added to the
z,Y   byte given as second in the instruction and the result used as the low order byte of a page zero address. For example, LDX $51,Y (code B6 51). If Y = $E9 then X will be given the value found in $003A (=$0000 + $51 + $E9).

(z,X)   *Pre-indexed indirect.* Tricky! An address is calculated as in the zero page indexed mode z,X. The values stored at z,X and z,X+1 are then used as the address where the data acted on is stored. Remember that z,X and z,X+1 are both in page zero which is used on a wraparound basis so that $0000 will follow $00FF. For example, STA ($A4,X) (code 81 A4). If X = $5B, then z,X = $00FF and z,X+1 = $0000. If $00FF contains $05 and $0000 contains $B2 then the value in the accumulator will be stored at $B205.

(z),Y   *Post-indexed indirect.* Trickier! The value in Y is added to an address contained in memory at z and z+1 to give the address of the data used. Remember that if z is $00FF then z+1 is $0000. The addition of Y is not on an 8-bit wraparound basis. For example, CMP ($A4),Y (code D1 A4). If $00A4 contains $A6 and $00A5 contains $38 and Y = $C0 then the value found at location $3966 (= $38A6 + $00C0) will be subtracted from the value in A and the N, Z and C flags will show the result but A will remain unchanged.

Other addressing modes used by the 6502 include *implied* which means that you do not have to give any data or address (e.g. TAX – Transfer A to X), *accumulator* which acts only on the accumulator (e.g. ASL A – arithmetic shift left accumulator) and *program relative* which is that used by the branch instructions where the second byte is used as an offset from the current program position as the destination of a jump.

Care must be taken when using indirect modes. The two memory bytes which store the address actually used must not cross a page boundary. In such a case, the 6502 will not pick up the correct address. It is safest to store addresses to be used indirectly at even byte locations.

Table headings, abbreviations and symbols

Mnemonic	Three-letter acronym of the operation performed (e.g. BCS is Branch if Carry Set) which an assembler will translate into machine code.
Action	A description of what an instruction will cause the processor to do.
Time	Time states. The execution time of each instruction in system clock cycles. A 6502 running at 1 MHz uses up one million Time states every second.
Code	The machine code of each instruction given as one, two or three pairs of hexadecimal (hex) digits. (For lo, lo hi, db or sd, you have to give the data or address you need.)
Status	Any flags changed by an instruction (see *flags*).
Mode	Different ways of pointing to data held in memory (see *addressing modes*).
db	Data byte. 8 bits of immediate data written into the program. It may be signed (-128 to $+127$) or unsigned (0 to 255) depending on use.
lo	Low order byte. The lowest 8 bits of a 16-bit address. Usually the address is in page zero and the processor assumes that the high order byte is $00.
lo hi	A 16-bit address. The 6502 needs this to be written with the low order byte before the high order byte.
m	Signifies a data byte held in memory or in the accumulator and accessed by means of one of the addressing modes.
m_n	Signifies bit n (n $=$ 0 to 7) of the data byte indicated by m.
PC_{lo}, PC_{hi}	Signifies the low and high order bytes of the program counter.

sd	Signed displacement. An 8-bit offset to the program counter used by branch instructions. Positive (forward) if bit $7 = 0$ (i.e. in the range 0 to 127). Negative if bit $7 = 1$ (i.e. in the range -1 to -128). The offset is from the address of the byte following the 2-byte branch instruction (see *PC*).
$\leftarrow$ and $\rightarrow$	Data (a bit, byte or 16-bit address) is moved or assigned in the direction of the arrow.
$\wedge$	Logical AND (see below).
$\vee$	Logical INCLUSIVE-OR (see below).
$\veebar$	Logical EXCLUSIVE-OR (see below).

AND, OR and EOR operate on corresponding individual bits only in the following way:

a	b	a $\wedge$ b	a $\vee$ b	a $\veebar$ b
0	0	0	0	0
0	1	0	1	1
1	0	0	1	1
1	1	1	1	0

A.1 Interrupt and Program Control

Mnemonic	*Action*	*Time*	*Status*	*Code*
JMP ab	$PC \leftarrow ab$	3	none	4C lo hi
JMP (ab)	$PC_{lo} \leftarrow (ab)$ $PC_{hi} \leftarrow (ab+1)$	5	none	6C lo hi
JSR ab	$PC \leftarrow PC - 1$	6	none	20 lo hi
	$(S) \leftarrow PC_{hi}$ $S \leftarrow S - 1$			
	$(S) \leftarrow PC_{lo}$ $S \leftarrow S - 1$			
	$PC \leftarrow ab$			
RTS	$S \leftarrow S + 1$ $PC_{lo} \leftarrow (S)$	6	none	60
	$S \leftarrow S + 1$ $PC_{hi} \leftarrow (S)$			
	$PC \leftarrow PC + 1$			
RTI	$S \leftarrow S + 1$ $P \leftarrow (S)$	6	all	40
	$S \leftarrow S + 1$ $PC_{lo} \leftarrow (S)$			
	$S \leftarrow S + 1$ $PC_{hi} \leftarrow (S)$			
BRK	$PC \leftarrow PC + 1$	7	BI	00
	$(S) \leftarrow PC_{hi}$ $S \leftarrow S - 1$			
	$(S) \leftarrow PC_{lo}$ $S \leftarrow S - 1$			
	$(S) \leftarrow P$ $S \leftarrow S - 1$			
	$PC_{lo} \leftarrow (FFFE)$ $PC_{hi} \leftarrow (FFFF)$			
	$B \leftarrow 1$ $I \leftarrow 1$			
NOP	no operation	2	none	EA

A.2 Status Control

Mnemonic	*Action*		*Time*	*Status*	*Code*
CLC	$C \leftarrow 0$	(clear carry)	2	C	18
SEC	$C \leftarrow 1$	(set carry)	2	C	38
CLI	$I \leftarrow 0$	(enable interrupts)	2	I	58
SEI	$I \leftarrow 1$	(disable interrupts)	2	I	78
CLV	$V \leftarrow 0$	(clear overflow flag)	2	V	B8
CLD	$D \leftarrow 0$	(binary mode)	2	D	D8
SED	$D \leftarrow 1$	(decimal mode)	2	D	F8

A.3 Conditional Branching

Mnemonic	Action	Time	Status	Code
BPL sd	If N = 0 then PC ← PC + sd	2	none	10 sd
BMI sd	If N = 1 then PC ← PC + sd	2	none	30 sd
BVC sd	If V = 0 then PC ← PC + sd	2	none	50 sd
BVS sd	If V = 1 then PC ← PC + sd	2	none	70 sd
BCC sd	If C = 0 then PC ← PC + sd	2	none	90 sd
BCS sd	If C = 1 then PC ← PC + sd	2	none	B0 sd
BNE sd	If Z = 0 then PC ← PC + sd	2	none	D0 sd
BEQ sd	If Z = 1 then PC ← PC + sd	2	none	F0 sd

Time given is for no branch. If branch occurs add one time state. If branch to another page (PC hi-byte affected) add another time state.

A.4 Register Transfer

Mnemonic	Action	Time	Status	Code
TYA	A ← Y	2	NZ	98
TAY	Y ← A	2	NZ	A8
TXA	A ← X	2	NZ	8A
TAX	X ← A	2	NZ	AA
TXS	S ← X	2	none	9A
TSX	X ← S	2	NZ	BA

A.5 Register Increment/Decrement

Mnemonic	Action	Time	Status	Code
INY	Y ← Y + 1	2	NZ	C8
INX	X ← X + 1	2	NZ	E8
DEY	Y ← Y − 1	2	NZ	88
DEX	X ← X − 1	2	NZ	CA

A.6 Stack

Mnemonic	Action	Time	Status	Code
PHP	(S) ← P S ← S − 1	3	none	08
PLP	S ← S + 1 P ← (S)	4	all	28
PHA	(S) ← A S ← S − 1	3	none	48
PLA	S ← S + 1 A ← (S)	4	NZ	68

A.7(a) Accumulator – Memory. Action and Status Change.

Mnemonic	Action	Status
ORA m	$A \leftarrow A \vee m$	NZ
AND m	$A \leftarrow A \wedge m$	NZ
EOR m	$A \leftarrow A \veebar m$	NZ
ADC m	$A \leftarrow A + m + C$	NVZC
STA m	$m \leftarrow A$	none
LDA m	$A \leftarrow m$	NZ
CMP m	$P \leftarrow \text{status}(A + \bar{m} + 1)$	NZC
SBC m	$A \leftarrow A + \bar{m} + C$	NVZC
BIT m	$Z \leftarrow \text{status}(A \wedge m)$ $N \leftarrow m_7$ $V \leftarrow m_6$	NVZ

$\bar{m}$ is the one's complement of m (i.e. m $\veebar$ $FF).

The zero flag Z is not valid after an arithmetic operation in decimal mode.

A.7(b) Accumulator – Memory. Time States and Code by Address Mode.

Mode:	(z,X)	z	#	ab	(z),Y	z,X	ab,Y	ab,X
Time:	6	3	2	4	6*	4	5*	5*
ORA	01 lo	05 lo	09 db	0D lo hi	11 lo	15 lo	19 lo hi	1D lo hi
AND	21 lo	25 lo	29 db	2D lo hi	31 lo	35 lo	39 lo hi	3D lo hi
EOR	41 lo	45 lo	49 db	4D lo hi	51 lo	55 lo	59 lo hi	5D lo hi
ADC	61 lo	65 lo	69 db	6D lo hi	71 lo	75 lo	79 lo hi	7D lo hi
STA	81 lo	85 lo	–	8D lo hi	91 lo	95 lo	99 lo hi	9D lo hi
LDA	A1 lo	A5 lo	A9 db	AD lo hi	B1 lo	B5 lo	B9 lo hi	BD lo hi
CMP	C1 lo	C5 lo	C9 db	CD lo hi	D1 lo	D5 lo	D9 lo hi	DD lo hi
SBC	E1 lo	E5 lo	E9 db	ED lo hi	F1 lo	F5 lo	F9 lo hi	FD lo hi
BIT	–	24 lo	–	2C lo hi	–	–	–	–

* Except for STA which always operates in the given times, subtract one time state if the addition of Y or X to the 16-bit address has no effect on the address hi-byte (i.e. no page change).

A.8(a) Index Register – Memory. Action and Status Change.

Mnemonic	*Action*	*Status*
STY m	m ← Y	none
STX m	m ← X	none
LDY m	Y ← m	NZ
LDX m	X ← m	NZ
CPY m	P ← status$(Y + \bar{m} + 1)$	NZC
CPX m	P ← status$(X + \bar{m} + 1)$	NZC

$\bar{m}$ is the one's complement of m (i.e. $\bar{m} \; \forall \; \$FF$).

A.8(b) Index Register – Memory. Time States and Code by Address Mode.

Mode:	#	z	ab	z,X	z,Y	ab,X	ab,Y
Time:	2	3	4	4	4	5*	5*
STY	–	84 lo	8C lo hi	94 lo	–	–	–
STX	–	86 lo	8E lo hi	–	96 lo	–	–
LDY	A0 db	A4 lo	AC lo hi	B4 lo	–	BC lo hi	–
LDX	A2 db	A6 lo	AE lo hi	–	B6 lo	–	BE lo hi
CPY	C0 db	C4 lo	CC lo hi	–	–	–	–
CPX	E0 db	E4 lo	EC lo hi	–	–	–	–

* Subtract one time state if the addition of X or Y to the 16-bit address has no effect on the address hi-byte (i.e. no page change).

A.9(a) Memory (and Accumulator). Action and Status Change.

Mnemonic	Action	Status
ASL m	$C \leftarrow m_7 \sim m_0 \leftarrow 0$	NZC
ROL m	$C \leftarrow m_7 \sim m_0 \leftarrow C$	NZC
LSR m	$0 \rightarrow m_7 \sim m_0 \rightarrow C$	NZC
ROR m	$C \rightarrow m_7 \sim m_0 \rightarrow C$	NZC
DEC m	$m \leftarrow m - 1$	NZ
INC m	$m \leftarrow m + 1$	NZ

$m_7 \sim m_0$ indicates that all bits are shifted by one place left or right.

A.9(b) Memory (and Accumulator). Time States and Code by Address Mode.

Mode:	A	z	ab	z,X	ab,X
Time:	2	5	6	6	7
ASL	0A	06 lo	0E lo hi	16 lo	1E lo hi
ROL	2A	26 lo	2E lo hi	36 lo	3E lo hi
LSR	4A	46 lo	4E lo hi	56 lo	5E lo hi
ROR	6A	66 lo	6E lo hi	76 lo	7E lo hi
DEC	–	C6 lo	CE lo hi	D6 lo	DE lo hi
INC	–	E6 lo	EE lo hi	F6 lo	FE lo hi

Appendix B
Binary and Hexadecimal Number Systems

The unit of information in a computer is a *binary digit*, called a *bit*, because this can have only two states, represented by 0 and 1, and two state electronic devices are the cheapest and most reliable in operation. Binary digits are grouped together to represent machine code instructions, numbers, characters or any non-standard meanings you care to assign to them.

Table B.1 Decimal, binary and hexadecimal representation.

Decimal	Binary (bit 3210) (value 8421)	Hexadecimal
0	0000	0
1	0001	1
2	0010	2
3	0011	3
4	0100	4
5	0101	5
6	0110	6
7	0111	7
8	1000	8
9	1001	9
10	1010	A
11	1011	B
12	1100	C
13	1101	D
14	1110	E
15	1111	F

In our *denary* or *decimal* (base 10) numbers, a digit can represent a value from 0 to 9. When a value of 10 occurs, the digit becomes 0 and the digit to the left of it, the next most significant digit, is increased by one. In binary (base 2) numbers, a digit can represent a value of 0 or 1. When a value of 2 occurs, the digit becomes 0 and the next most significant digit is increased by one, i.e. a 0 becomes 1 or a 1 becomes 0 and the next most significant digit again is increased by one, and so on.

It takes many 0's and 1's in the binary system to represent a high value and so they are usually expressed in *hexadecimal* (base 16) numbers, where each hexadecimal digit represents four binary digits. Table B.1 showing the first sixteen numbers, in decimal, binary and hexadecimal, will make this clear.

Bit 3 is the most significant and bit 0 the least significant digit of the binary number. A one in the bit zero position has a value of 1, in the bit one position a value of 2, in the bit two position a value of 4 and in the bit three position a value of 8. A single hexadecimal digit can represent a value up to 15 and, since we have no single numbers to represent values higher than 9, the letters A - F are used to represent values 10 to 15. To show that they are hexadecimal, these numbers are often preceded by a '$'. For example, $20 is the hexadecimal number 20, having a value of decimal 32.

It can be seen in Table B.1 that all our decimal digits 0 to 9 can be accommodated in 4 bits. That is half the space needed for the ASCII characters nought to nine, which are coded $30 to $39. Decimal digits can therefore be packed two to a byte and, in this form, are known as BCD (binary coded decimal) digits. The 6502 has two special instructions, SED and CLD, and the D flag to allow arithmetic to be done with numbers in this form. This will be seen in Chapters 9 and 10.

A group of 8 bits is known as a byte. As the 6502 provides for eight data lines, the byte, representing 8 binary digits, 2 hexadecimal digits, 2 BCD digits, an ASCII character, an unsigned decimal value up to 255 or an 8-bit code of some kind, is the most common grouping. Another common grouping is that of two bytes, referred to as a *word*, as the 6502 provides 16 lines for addresses.

A decimal number is converted to binary by successively dividing it by two, until the decimal value is zero, and using the remainders as the binary digits. Figure B.1 shows such a conversion.

```
2 | 2 5        Remainder
2 | 1 2        1        least significant digit
2 |  6         0
2 |  3         0
2 |  1         1
     0         1        most significant digit
```

Decimal 2 5 = binary 1 1 0 0 1

Fig. B.1. Decimal to binary conversion.

A binary number can be converted to decimal by adding up the value of each binary column in which a bit is set (see under 'Binary' in Table B.1). Another method is to double the most significant bit of the number and add the result to the bit on its right. The result of this addition is doubled and added to the next bit. The process is repeated until the addition into the least significant bit. Take, for example, binary digit 11001. The most significant digit is doubled and added into the next digit, giving 3. Three is doubled and added into the next digit, giving 6. Six is doubled and added into the next digit, giving 12. Twelve is doubled and added into the least significant digit, giving 25.

An 8-bit binary number can represent a value of 255, if all the bits are set. Add up the value of each binary column (1, 2, 4, 8, 16, 32, 64, 128) and see. In machine code, the programmer decides what a byte represents and deals with it in the program accordingly. But this arrangement can only apply where all numbers are positive and do not need to be signed. When a number can be either positive or negative, the most significant bit (bit 7 in a byte, bit 15 in a word, bit 23 in a 3-byte number or whatever) is used as the sign bit — with a zero indicating a positive, and a one indicating a negative number. An 8-bit signed binary number can represent values from minus 128 to plus 127.

6502 Arithmetic instructions operate on what are known as *2's complement binary numbers*. Take the signed binary number having a decimal value of five, 0101. The 1's complement of this (all the bits reversed) is 1010. Adding the two together gives 1111, which is not zero; therefore 1010 cannot be minus five. The 2's complement of a number will, when added to the number, reset all result bits to zero, ignoring the carry beyond the most significant end. It is, in fact, the number subtracted from zero or the 1's complement of the number + 1 and the 2's complement of five (minus five) is binary 1011. The general rule to get the 2's complement of a signed binary number — whether it is negative or positive to start with — is: starting with the least significant bit, leave all bits unchanged up to and including the first set (1) bit and reverse all the other bits.

Appendix C
ASCII Character Codes

Hex	Chr	Hex	Chr	Hex	Chr
00	NUL	1C	FS	38	8
01	SOH	1D	GS	39	9
02	STX	1E	RS	3A	:
03	ETX	1F	US	3B	;
04	EOT	20	SP	3C	<
05	ENQ	21	!	3D	=
06	ACK	22	"	3E	>
07	BEL	23	#	3F	?
08	BS	24	$	40	@
09	HT	25	%	41	A
0A	LF	26	&	42	B
0B	VT	27	'	43	C
0C	FF	28	(	44	D
0D	CR	29	)	45	E
0E	SO	2A	*	46	F
0F	SI	2B	+	47	G
10	DLE	2C	,	48	H
11	DC1	2D	—	49	I
12	DC2	2E	.	4A	J
13	DC3	2F	/	4B	K
14	DC4	30	0	4C	L
15	NAK	31	1	4D	M
16	SYN	32	2	4E	N
17	ETB	33	3	4F	O
18	CAN	34	4	50	P
19	EM	35	5	51	Q
1A	SUB	36	6	52	R
1B	ESC	37	7	53	S

Hex	*Chr*	*Hex*	*Chr*	*Hex*	*Chr*
54	T	63	c	72	r
55	U	64	d	73	s
56	V	65	e	74	t
57	W	66	f	75	u
58	X	67	g	76	v
59	Y	68	h	77	w
5A	Z	69	i	78	x
5B	[	6A	j	79	y
5C	\	6B	k	7A	z
5D	]	6C	l	7B	{
5E	^	6D	m	7C	|
5F	_	6E	n	7D	}
60	'	6F	o	7E	~
61	a	70	p	7F	DEL
62	b	71	q		

NUL	Null	DC1	Device control 1
SOH	Start of heading	DC2	Device control 2
STX	Start of text	DC3	Device control 3
ETX	End of text	DC4	Device control 4
EOT	End of transmission	NAK	Negative acknowledge
ENQ	Enquiry	SYN	Synchronous idle
ACK	Acknowledge	ETB	End of transmission block
BEL	Bell or alarm	CAN	Cancel
BS	Backspace	EM	End of medium
HT	Horizontal tabulation	SUB	Substitute
LF	Line feed	ESC	Escape
VT	Vertical tabulation	FS	File separator
FF	Form feed	GS	Group separator
CR	Carriage return	RS	Record separator
SO	Shift out	US	Unit separator
SI	Shift in	SP	Space
DLE	Data link escape	DEL	Delete

Index of Routines

Index

The index manuscript was produced using Owen Bishop's program, *Indexer*, adapted for the BBC Micro. (Ref: *Computing Today*, Vol. 5, No.4, June 1983.)